redefining the
STRONG-
WILLED
WOMAN

cynthia ulrich tobias

redefining the
STRONG-
WILLED
WOMAN

How to Effectively Use Your Strong Will for God

ZONDERVAN™

GRAND RAPIDS, MICHIGAN 49530 USA

ZONDERVAN™

Redefining the Strong-Willed Woman
Copyright © 2002 by Cynthia Ulrich Tobias

Requests for information should be addressed to:

Zondervan, *Grand Rapids, Michigan 49530*

Library of Congress Cataloging-in-Publication Data
Tobias, Cynthia Ulrich, 1953–
   Redefining the strong-willed woman : how to effectively use your strong will
for God / Cynthia Ulrich Tobias.
      p. cm.
   Includes bibliographical references (p.   ).
   ISBN 0-310-24578-8
   1. Christian women—Religious life. 2. Christian women—Conduct of life.
I. Title.
BV4527.T62 2002
248.8'43—dc21   2002008519
                                                   CIP

This edition printed on acid-free paper.

All Scripture quotations, unless otherwise indicated, are taken from THE MESSAGE.
Copyright © by Eugene H. Peterson 1993, 1994, 1995. Used by permission of Nav-
Press Publishing Group.

Scripture quotations marked KJV are taken from the King James version of the Bible.

Published in association with the literary agency of Alive Communications, Inc., 7680
Goddard Street, Suite 200, Colorado Springs, CO 80920.

Interior design by Beth Shagene

Printed in the United States of America

02 03 04 05 06 07 08 /❖ DC/ 10 9 8 7 6 5 4 3 2 1

Contents

Acknowledgments

I owe a debt of gratitude to so many! In addition to my husband, John, and our sons, Mike and Robert, my mother, Minnie Ulrich, has worked tirelessly with me in my business for over fifteen years. She made sure I had the time and space to write this book, and worried more about the deadlines than even I did! My other office staff—Juanita Davis and Flo Tiemann—have put up with a lot of distractions while I finished this important project. My literary agent, Linda Glasford, and Alive Communications gave me encouragement and guidance, and I enjoy our professional relationship. My editor, Sandra Vander Zicht, somehow made me feel that all her suggestions were only minor adjustments, even though every time she worked with me the manuscript came out stronger.

I especially want to thank Kathy Perry, a good friend and classic strong-willed woman who serves God in her ministry and who has been a wonderful sounding board throughout this entire undertaking. Kathy helped me establish an incredibly helpful strong-willed women one-another group, whose members shared powerful stories and invaluable insights. I want to personally thank those women: Jackie Myers, Carol Sheldahl, Paula Gerstmann, Janna Johnson, and Diane Johnson. They stand as vivid examples of how strong-willed women can bring honor and glory to God.

Introduction

*God can do anything, you know—far more than you
could ever imagine or guess or request in your wildest
dreams! He does it not by pushing us around but by
working within us, his Spirit deeply and gently within us.*
—Ephesians 3:20

It was a well-attended conference for Christian women, and I
sat in the huge ballroom among dozens of tables with neatly
dressed ladies who were eager to hear the keynote speaker.
Before the nationally recognized author was introduced, the
hostess said, "We're going to have a little activity to help us get
to know each other." My smile froze, and I quickly scanned the
room for the nearest exit.

"No offense," I whispered to my neighbor, "but I hate these
'ice breaker' activities."

She looked surprised and slightly offended, but I had my eye
on the volunteers headed toward us bringing cute little gift bas-
kets full of fortune cookies and blank pieces of paper. I excused
myself and walked past several disapproving glances as I escaped
through the double doors. I stood outside the ballroom during
the introductory activity, then slipped back into the rear of the
room in time to hear the speaker.

Uh oh—I was in trouble. She was speaking in a soft, sing-song voice, and I suddenly felt like a first grader again. I tried to focus on what she was saying; her personal testimony was interesting, and many in the room, including me, were moved to tears. But then she began to tell us how we can become more godly women, and I once again found myself tuning out. It's not that I disagreed with her scripturally based instruction, and I honestly wasn't trying to find fault with her delivery style. But she didn't seem to have much in common with me. I couldn't help thinking she tended to give in too easily when she described the challenges in her life. She seemed eager to cook and clean for her husband and family and considered it a joy just to be able to serve in her kids' school and her local church. Nothing wrong with that, of course, but I kept waiting for her to say something that would compel me to think about God as something besides a deity who wanted me to be a submissive and quiet woman.

Several months later, I attended a very different kind of women's conference. This one was sponsored by a high-profile secular university and had several corporate cosponsors. The display tables included information on NOW (National Organization of Women) and opportunities to donate to Planned Parenthood. The attendees were primarily businesswomen looking for ways to scale the ladder of success and gain new confidence in corporate boardrooms. I sensed immediately that this would not be anything like the warm and welcoming Christian women's conference. These speakers seemed ruthless, and the spirit of competition was fierce. I ended up walking out of this conference early too, but for an entirely different reason.

The speaker I was listening to was articulate and spoke in a firm, commanding voice, but her message troubled me. She told us she had been given the once-in-a-lifetime opportunity to meet a celebrity she had always admired. He had actually spent time talking to her and giving her some advice, and she couldn't wait to tell her husband about what had happened. Her husband's reaction was less than enthusiastic, she said, and he told her the celebrity probably told everyone the same thing. "I couldn't believe he could be so unsupportive of me!" she exclaimed, then added, "Well, that was it—I'd had it. You know what I did? I divorced him!" The room broke out in spontaneous applause. Whoa—I didn't have much in common with *these* women!

I realized I do not fit into either group of women. I am not a quiet, unassuming woman who is content to simply blend in and become the silent partner for her husband's success. Neither am I a loud, in-your-face female who believes men need to be conquered and put in their place. I do have a strong will and firm convictions. I'm not afraid to speak my mind, and when I am committed to accomplishing a goal, I'll move heaven and earth to get the job done. I've gotten in trouble more than once for being too pushy, and I've unintentionally offended others who thought I simply railroaded them into doing what I wanted. I am not afraid to take risks, and I don't have much patience for people who won't try to make their lives better without depending on someone else to do it for them.

I know I'm not alone. Over almost two decades of public speaking, I've met thousands of women like me. I've discovered, however, that it takes some coaxing to get them to admit it. For some it takes more convincing than others. You see, especially in Christian circles, we're a little reluctant to come right out and say we're strong willed and proud of it. We've somehow been persuaded that God would not approve of a woman who is so, well, nonconforming. After all, isn't the virtuous woman supposed to be quiet, holy, and subservient? I actually had one older Christian woman tell me when I was a young adult that when we accept Christ as our Savior, he *neutralizes* us. Now there's a scary thought!

The fact is, the single most important thing any of us will *ever* do is accept Jesus Christ as our personal Savior. But God himself created and designed us before we were even born. He gave us our personalities, our gifts, our learning styles, and our individual passions and desires. When I turn my life back over to him, what happens to my natural drive and ambition? What do I do with my fiercely competitive spirit or my adventurous heart? Sadly, too many women decide they cannot possibly keep their strong will and still be considered a "good girl." They try to fit into the mold of compliance and submission in order to be accepted and valued. Too often they end up either being emotionally confused or turning their backs on a God who seems entirely too narrow and controlling.

But there are many godly women who still hold on to a healthy strong-willed spirit and have dedicated their strength and energy to the kingdom. They are sometimes misunderstood and are often perceived as being a little too outspoken or bold. But our churches and families are sprinkled liberally with fine women who, like their compliant counterparts, bring love and discipline and nurturing to all who come under their influence. This book is first and foremost dedicated to these women. I want you to know you are not the only one out there who feels the way you do. There are hundreds of thousands of sisters in Christ who share your perspectives and your convictions. There are untold thousands of younger strong-willed women who are craving your knowledge, support, and mentorship.

This book is also dedicated to the strong-willed women who, until now, have been afraid to admit it, and to the "bad girls" who have always wondered why God can't have more fun or be more flexible. The way to salvation is indeed narrow, but service to our Lord is broader than we can imagine. God *does* require that we surrender our strong will completely to him. But what he gives back is an incredible transformation of our carnal spirit into a glorious nature that actually intensifies our inborn strengths. We aren't really giving up anything, except being eternally lost. We can challenge what we may have been told in the past about how a "proper" Christian woman behaves. We can find ourselves right in the center of God's will and still be doing what we do best—using our strong wills to bring honor and glory to him.

Sprinkled throughout the book, you will find the thoughts of other strong-willed women. "In Her Own Words" will give you just a small glimpse inside the minds and hearts of other women who may be very much like you. At the end of this book there is a study and discussion guide designed to help you apply what you will discover and give you opportunities to discuss your ideas with kindred spirits.

One of my favorite stories is "The Lion and the Christian." This poor Christian man is running from a lion, and he knows he is losing the race. As the lion gains ground, the exhausted Christian finally gives up and leans against a tree, facing the charging beast. The Christian raises his hand and calls loudly, "Lord! Make this lion a Christian!" Amazingly, the animal instantly falls to his knees and begins to pray: "O Lord, thank you for this meal I am about to partake." That's right—you can make a lion a Christian, but do you know what? He's still a lion. It is my prayer that this book will help you attach a whole new meaning to the worn-out phrase "I am woman; hear me roar." God is about to give you the courage to be a strong-willed lion for him!

part 1

What Is
a Strong-Willed
Woman?

chapter 1

Who Is the Strong-Willed Woman?

It is clear to us, friends, that God not only loves you very much but also has put his hand on you for something special. When the Message we preached came to you, it wasn't just words. Something happened in you. The Holy Spirit put steel in your convictions.

—1 Thessalonians 1:4–5

A pleasant, petite Texan was introducing me to an audience of several hundred women at Baylor University, where I was speaking about strong-willed children. The moderator had obviously been a strong-willed child. With a gentle southern drawl, she grinned and winked at the audience. "My mother always used to tell me I was the only one of my kind—in captivity."

I had to smile. What a great way to put it! I was only one of at least two hundred other strong-willed daughters in that crowd who immediately knew what her mother had meant. We look for opportunities to stand out from the herd, so to speak. We resist being lumped together, even if we share the label of strong-willed women. We are as diverse from one another as we are unique in the world. Our strong will doesn't take the place of personality, temperament, or learning style. It frames each of our souls, providing the border for hundreds of puzzle pieces, including spiritual gifts, personal preferences, childhood and life experiences. Although we differ in many ways, we *can* forge strong bonds with each other by identifying and affirming the strengths we have in common. The woman who alphabetizes her spice cabinet and color codes the hangers in her closet can be just as strong willed as the woman who writes out checks according to the pictures she likes and keeps her stuff in piles instead of files.

So what does it take to have the distinction of being a genuinely strong-willed woman? After all, every woman has opportunities to use some degree of strong will at various times in her life. Much of what we'll share in this book could characterize almost any woman when she's backed into a corner or forced to protect the ones she loves. But for those of us who fit the description of the strong-willed woman, it can be said that we use our strong wills almost as often as we breathe. It is so deeply ingrained in us we often struggle to understand why everyone doesn't share the depth and strength of our convictions.

I met Emily after one of my learning styles seminars for public school teachers. She had not grown up in a Christian home, but she had attended a conservative church off and on during her youth. She thanked me, not only for the seminar but for weaving my faith into the presentation. Then she hesitantly asked me, "Do you believe it's even possible for a strong-willed woman to be a Christian?" I was startled by the question, and she went on to confess that she had very deliberately stayed away from

In Her Own Words

At times in my life I questioned God for making me so strong willed. This strong will had taken on a life of its own and seemed more of a burden than a blessing. How could I feel so strongly about so many things? It took years to come to terms with this, but I now realize that my strong will is one of the most treasured gifts the Lord has given me, and I thank him daily for entrusting this to me!
— MKMKSMITH

church the past few years because she knew she had a stubborn and independent nature. Half of her was afraid God wouldn't even want her, and the other half was afraid he would demand she give up her strong will if she did decide to give her heart to Christ. Emily is certainly not alone. There are so many strong-willed women whose hearts and souls long to know Christ but whose self-sufficient natures won't even consider the possibility of surrendering their hard-won independence. These are women who can and will change the world—one way or another—and it's never been more important to find a way to recognize and validate their worth in the kingdom of God.

Many of us may have secretly wondered if there was something wrong with us, if perhaps we just weren't trying hard enough to be good conforming Christian women. So let's come together and identify ourselves to each other and the world. Let's discover and celebrate the fact that God has placed in the heart of many of his human creations an undercurrent so strong and so solid it carries us from birth to death.

How Strong-Willed Are You?

The following is a quick, informal quiz to get a handle on how strong willed you are according to how we'll be defining it in this book. Answer honestly, understanding that strong will itself is *not* a negative trait; it only *becomes* negative when you use it in ways that do not honor God. After you take and score the quiz, have at least two other people who know you best take it on your behalf, just to see if their scores match yours.

Your SWW (Strong-Willed Woman) Quotient

Place a mark in front of each of the following statements that almost always describe you.

____ When told to give up because it's impossible, I'm willing to move heaven and earth to prove you wrong.

____ I can move with lightning speed from being a warm, loving presence to being a cold, immovable force.

____ I may argue the point into the ground, sometimes just to see how far into the ground the point will go.

____ When given the ultimatum "Do it or else," I will often just "else."

____ I consider rules to be guidelines. (I'm abiding by the spirit of the law; why are you being so picky?)

____ I can show great creativity and resourcefulness; I always seem to find a way to accomplish the goal.

____ I can turn what seems to be the smallest issue into a grand crusade or a raging controversy.

____ I don't do things just because "you're supposed to"; it needs to matter to me personally.

____ I usually refuse to obey unconditionally; I almost always have a few terms of negotiation before complying.

____ I'm not afraid to try the unknown, to conquer the unfamiliar (but I'll choose my own risks).

____ I've been told I can take what was meant to be the simplest request and interpret it as an offensive ultimatum.

____ I may not say the exact words to apologize, but I do make things right.

Your Score: How Much Strong Will Do You Have?

0–3   You've got it, but you don't use it much.

4–7   You use it when you need to, but not on a daily basis.

8–10   You've got a good strong dose of it, but you can back off when you want to.

11–12   You don't leave home without it, and it's almost impossible not to use it.

If you scored between 11 and 12, you have definitely come to the right place! Your heart will instantly warm to the discussions of how we think and why we do the things we do. You have found your kindred spirits!

If your score is between 8 and 10, you may not be completely sure we are describing you when we talk about some of the more extreme traits of the strong-willed woman. As you read through the book, the chances are good you will discover you have more strong will than you thought, but perhaps—for a lot of reasons—you haven't felt free to admit it openly. The chapters you are about to read may liberate and empower you more than you expected.

If you scored between 1 and 7, you are probably reading this book to gain a better understanding of the strong-willed women in your life, and we certainly encourage your efforts. We are not really a mystery, but most of us will tell you it takes one to know one, and understanding us can be a challenge.

What Do Strong-Willed Women Have in Common?

You've probably figured out that I scored a 12 on the quiz you just took. I have to confess that throughout these pages I will be speaking directly to those who think like I do—and believe me, that's no small number of women! As we identify what most of us have in common, you will find this is by no means a comprehensive list. But it can start the important process of understanding and appreciating what can make strong-willed women such a powerful and positive force in the kingdom of God.

Read the following descriptions carefully and prayerfully. The positive characteristics can be true of any strong-willed woman. It is my heartfelt belief, however, that only through God's grace can any strong-willed woman avoid the negative aspects of even our best traits. Several of these characteristics will be explored in more detail later in the book, but this will give you an overview of what almost all strong-willed women have in common. Is this *your* heart? Does this describe so much of your innermost being? Are you a part of this unique and wonderful group of godly women?

I Have a Deep Desire to Make a Difference

Deep in my heart, there is a desire to make a difference. I am not content to simply blend in with the crowd. I want to do something significant, something extraordinary. It may not shake the whole world, but I want to make sure my corner of it is never the same.

How this can take the wrong direction: Before God transforms my will, I run the risk of alienating others. I can start finding any way possible to be different, to ensure that I do not conform to the expectations of those I often resent for dictating the rules to me in the first place.

I Am Not Content to Coast

I am not content to simply coast; I must keep pedaling. Laziness certainly does not appear to be a trait that shows up among strong-willed women. In fact, if anything, most of us chafe under the constraints of waiting for just about anything. Isn't there something I can do to move things along? Shouldn't *someone* be doing *something?* Let's take action!

How this can take the wrong direction: I can live in a consistent state of impatience with just about everything and almost everyone. I can find myself snapping at others who won't move at my pace, and making unreasonable demands of those who love me best yet often understand me least.

I Am Fiercely Loyal

I am fiercely loyal—until betrayed. I will fight to the death to protect the weak and helpless or to advance a cause that does the same. But once my trust has been betrayed, the disconnection is swift and often permanent.

How this can take the wrong direction: I can easily be drawn to the wrong cause, and once I'm there I fight for it despite all evidence that I'm supporting the wrong thing. The more someone attempts to pull me away, the more adamant I become to stick with it, even if I secretly believe it *would* be best to disconnect.

I Need to Be Involved

I need to be involved, to become part of the solution to compelling problems. I am energized by the process of finding answers to problems no one else could solve. The idea that something is impossible only fuels my resolve to seek and discover the solution that will prove it was possible after all.

How this can take the wrong direction: I can step into situations without invitation and insinuate myself into circumstances in which I'm not really welcome. There's no such thing as "none of my business."

I Will Not Be Ignored

I will not be ignored when I believe I have something important to say. I will find a way to be heard, whether it is through print or public speaking. I don't just sit back and hope someone else will mention it eventually.

In Her Own Words

I will absolutely not give up on things once I put my mind to them: marriage, parenting, overcoming emotional difficulties, bad habits. I believe obstacles can be overcome, and faith in God just magnifies that a hundredfold.

—DCEALLAIGH

In Her Own Words

My strong will has sometimes gotten me in trouble because I am very opinionated and tend to say what I think before thinking it through; because of my "strong will," I have a hard time learning from my mistakes.

—NINELIVES

How this can take the wrong direction: I can become loud, obnoxious, or rude while demanding that others listen. Others may find their voices are drowned out in my all-encompassing need to be the one who talks.

I Have No Reverse Gear

I have no reverse gear—only drive. (I'll drive around the block to go backward.) Perhaps it's my overall philosophy of "what's done is done; let's move on." I don't try to go backward and undo the past. Even if I immediately sense I've made the wrong decision, I keep driving forward, looking for a way to make things right.

How this can take the wrong direction: I can live as though I am never wrong, never retreating, only advancing regardless of the price.

I Tend to Succeed

I tend to succeed at virtually everything I do, usually because I don't choose to do anything I believe doesn't promise certain success. It often seems to those watching that I am successful at almost everything I undertake. My secret is this: I choose what

I tackle very deliberately, going ahead with only the challenges I feel pretty confident I can overcome.

How this can take the wrong direction: I may refuse to do what God wants me to do, simply out of the fear that I'll look weak or incapable.

I Am Wholehearted in Action

Whatever I choose to do, I do with my whole heart. There aren't many halfway measures when it comes to the strong-willed woman. If I have decided to do a task, I usually throw myself into the effort wholeheartedly. Stand back!

How this can take the wrong direction: I can railroad through just about anyone and anything when I've set my sights on the goal, oblivious to those who may be hurt in the process.

I Have Diverse Interests

I have very diverse interests. I never want to be stuck in a job because I have no other choice. Most strong-willed women have held dozens of jobs, usually two or three simultaneously. I thrive by moving from the known to the unknown. I want to be able to do anything I need to, whenever I need to do it, and I believe that life's too short to be miserable in a job I hate.

How this can take the wrong direction: I can get the reputation of never holding down a job for any length of time. I can switch jobs when I get bored, regardless of who I'm letting down in the process.

I Have a Strong Desire to Do Right

I have a strong desire to do the right thing, with or without specific rules. I want you to assume the best in me. I have a deep-

---

In Her Own Words

When I was younger I would have denied being strong willed. I would have told you, "I'm passionate about my beliefs"; "I'm committed to a course of action"; "I can't do something I think is wrong."

While all those things are true, I now know that my strong will does have something to do with it. Now that I have a little more wisdom on my side, I'm more willing to let others learn through experience, and I don't always have to have my own way, but I'm still very "persuasive."

—LEANNE

---

seated desire to do the moral and decent thing in any situation. It's why rules are often simply "guidelines"; as long as I know the point of the rule, why must I follow every picky requirement?

How this can take the wrong direction: I can flaunt authority and run roughshod over those who insist I follow step-by-step procedures or explicit rules.

I Am Willing to Do What Needs to Be Done

I'm willing to step up and do what needs to be done, even if no one else has the courage to join me. Even if I lack training in a particular kind of crisis, I'm still willing to step out and do something while others look helplessly around wondering what to do. I am not content to stay behind the lines and wistfully wait for someone to rescue me.

How this can take the wrong direction: I may blunder into things like a bull in a china shop, regardless of the consequences. I may make others feel small or stupid because they didn't take the same risks I was willing to take.

What Do You Think?

Well, what do you think? Could it be that you have just read a pretty accurate description of yourself? Did you notice how easily our best qualities can become major drawbacks? I love being a strong-willed woman, but it's a daily challenge to walk that fine line between holy convictions and self-righteous pride.

I think you'll enjoy your journey in self-discovery over the next several chapters. I know you'll be encouraged to find out how many other women share your views and celebrate the fulfillment that can come only as a result of transforming that incredible strong will to the one who gave it to you in the first place. Watch out—you're about to change the world!

Prayer for Strong-Willed Women

We ask that our Heavenly Father take the very traits that have the potential to be negative and transform them into strengths that bring honor and glory to the Creator and Designer of our strong will.

chapter 2

Strong Will—
It's Not Always
What You Think!

*Now here's a surprise: The master praised the crooked
manager! And why? Because he knew how to look after
himself. Streetwise people are smarter in this regard than
law-abiding citizens. They are on constant alert, looking for
angles, surviving by their wits. I want you to be smart in
the same way—but for what is* right—*using every
adversity to stimulate you to creative survival, to concentrate
your attention on the bare essentials, so you'll live, really
live, and not complacently just get by on good behavior.*

—Luke 16: 8–9

When I was writing my book about strong-willed children
(You Can't Make Me—But I Can Be Persuaded), I would
ask friends and acquaintances if they had a strong-willed child.
Their responses were often defensive, assuming the worst: "Oh,
no—my son has never rebelled against us," or "My daughter is
a very good girl." It was more common to hear an affirmative
answer from parents who were at the end of their rope trying to
deal with children they didn't understand. "I have six children,"
one mother told me, "and they're all strong willed." The fact is,

strong will and rebellion or defiance are not synonymous. Being strong willed doesn't automatically mean one will be defiant or cause parents a lot of trouble. And children who make a parent's life challenging or difficult aren't necessarily strong willed.

Many of you reading this book have struggled with how you've been labeled since childhood. You may have had an authoritarian parent who insisted on unquestioned obedience and you were considered the troublemaker. Maybe your friends or classmates thought of you as demanding or bossy because you always wanted to be in charge. Perhaps some of your biggest battles were with teachers who so often seemed to force you to do work that was a waste of time. They thought you were just being lazy or rebellious. The chances are good that even now, as an adult, many of the people who love you most are still mystified by the way you act and think.

It's time to explode a few myths and commonly held beliefs when it comes to truly knowing and understanding the hearts and minds of strong-willed women. Let's just take what I consider to be the top five myths:

In Her Own Words

Growing up in a traditional Hispanic family, where women are not supposed to speak their own mind or, even worse, object to the opinions of the men in the family, has always created a problem for me. I was thought of as being the "difficult one." By voicing my opinions and choosing not be traditional in my family, my parents always said that I was stubborn and difficult.

— ANONYMOUS

Myth 1: A Strong Will Is Automatically a Negative Trait

When I was growing up, I would frequently get in trouble for what I considered my "gift of sarcasm." When you're younger, people don't really consider it a gift. In fact, there are lots of other less complimentary names for it: smart mouth, back talk, smart aleck. But when I got older, it suddenly came in very handy.

True to my nature, I have worked in many diverse jobs in my life. One summer early in my teaching career, I spent an evening as a "ride-along" with a police officer friend of mine. I was immediately hooked. I really wanted to try doing this job for a while! I figured out that as a fully commissioned reserve police officer, I could work full-time in the summers and part-time evenings and weekends during the school year.

So in the '80s I spent six years as a fully commissioned reserve police officer. In 1980, when I applied for the position, the department I chose had no female police officers. They were pretty clear during my interview that they weren't really eager to break tradition for my sake. I promised them I wasn't just trying to make a statement about gender equality; I asked for no special favors or consideration. But I really believed I could do a good job, and I passionately wanted the chance to prove it. One of the veteran officers frowned at me and said, "Didn't you grow up in kind of a 'goody two shoes' environment?"

I raised my eyebrows and replied, "Well, I guess. My dad's a preacher."

He nodded smugly. "So," he continued, "do you swear?"

I couldn't hide my surprise. "Oh, no," I told him, "we were not allowed to use profanity growing up."

He leaned closer to me. "Well how do you expect to get along with the bad guys if you don't talk like they do?"

I had no immediate reply, and he sat back into his chair. "I tell you what," he said. "We'll give you a chance. But I give you six months. In six months you'll be swearing like a longshoreman." He didn't know that he had just issued an irresistible challenge to a strong-willed woman.

As I undertook the duties of a cop, I found out my gift of sarcasm actually worked better than profanity. The bad guy would be in the holding cell while I was booking him in. He'd be yelling and screaming obscenities at me. I would stop, smile sweetly at him, and say, "I'm rubber and you're glue. Everything you say bounces off of me and sticks to you!"

That, of course, would only make him angrier, and he'd taunt me. "Oh, big woman cop, huh? Bet you hate all men."

I would look at him, smile again, and reply, "No, not normally, but in your case I'd be glad to make an exception."

In six years, I never once had to utter a word of profanity. Okay, I got in trouble a couple of times for a little too smart of a mouth. But the sarcasm—the very thing that was supposed to be one of my biggest drawbacks—was what helped keep me on the path of righteousness. Strong will is not automatically a negative trait. In fact, just the opposite is true.

Everyone needs at least some strong will in order to survive hardships, persevere through trials, and accomplish the impossible. Think of how many strong-willed men and women had to continue to hold their families together after the tragedy of the World Trade Center. So many children lost parents; thousands of parents were instantly thrust into unbearable grief at a time when they had to be the strongest for their children. How could they do it? Only the grace of God held them steady, and those who had the strongest wills found themselves called upon over and over to provide leadership and direction. Suddenly that iron will was the greatest asset for rescue and recovery workers who labored around the clock with grim determination. No one criticized their strong wills; everyone just prayed for sustained energy and commitment whatever the cost.

Strong will, to some degree, is needed at every age—for a child who is subjected to abuse or neglect, a woman who must battle breast cancer, a man who leads his troops into war. All must draw upon their reserve of strong will. Just think how blessed we are as strong-willed women to have so much of it in the first place!

Myth 2: Strong-Willed Women Are Man-Haters

One of the most unfortunate effects of the "women's liberation movement" was the opportunity for a small number of bitter, vindictive women to convince the media that a strong-willed woman could and should succeed without the help of a man. Men were represented as oppressors, chauvinist pigs, and a good old boys club. The familiar mantra "A woman without a man is like a fish without a bicycle" made it abundantly clear that battle lines were being drawn and enemies were being defined. Understandably, men began to be defensive and suspicious when they encountered a strong-willed, confident woman. Would she be angry if they held the door open? Would she charge sexual harassment if they engaged her in office banter? Where should they draw the line?

I have worked in several traditionally male-dominated jobs with great success. I have not asked for special favors or consideration. I want the standards to be held high. I couldn't respect myself or the organization if the qualifications had to be compromised in order for me to succeed.

For the six years I worked as a police officer, I wore a badge that identified me as "patrolman." That's okay—I didn't fight to get it changed or complain about the fact that I was the only woman on the police force in our municipality. I wasn't out to prove a woman could do a man's job. I just wanted to succeed in a profession I truly enjoyed. I endured a generous amount of teasing and a healthy dose of skepticism during my first year or two as a cop. I never expected my fellow officers to cut me any extra slack. By the same token, they didn't have to guess where the line was between good-natured teasing and harassment. We all worked hard at earning and maintaining mutual respect.

Respect is definitely a two-way street. The strong-willed Christian woman understands that you cannot harbor resentment, bitterness, or anger and still bring honor and glory to God. When it comes to dealing with men, most successful strategies work regardless of gender. The vast majority of strong-willed women already recognize that working to bring out the best in each person—man or woman—is a winning formula.

Myth 3: Strong-Willed Women Have Been, Are, or Will Be Rebellious "Bad Girls"

I have to admit I am not your classic bad girl who had a life-changing conversion after walking on the wild side. Sometimes

I've almost wished my personal story was more dramatic, but I came to know Christ early, and I was blessed with an incredibly loving and stable Christian home. My strong-willed father dedicated more than fifty years to full-time Christian ministry. Being a preacher's kid carries with it a whole host of potential opportunities for rebellion, but although my dad ruled the roost firmly and decisively, his heart toward my sister and me has always been loving and respectful. I grew up in a virtual Sodom and Gomorrah, attending junior high school in Reno, Nevada, and senior high in Las Vegas. I got a lot of what I call "spiritual field trips." When you are observing full-time ministry in Reno and Las Vegas, you get exposed to the underbelly of a corrupt and often frightening world. I knew almost as much about showgirls as I did about saints and met as many prostitutes as I did preachers. I got a firsthand look at the fruits of rebellion—alcoholism, gambling, drug addictions, and all sorts of criminal activities.

In adulthood, my experiences in law enforcement just reinforced my earlier decisions not to step over the line. God was

---

In Her Own Words

My strong will has been God's way of protecting me from bowing to peer pressure. I never felt inclined to drink, use drugs, act promiscuously, participate in all the new fads, or buy into a particular party line. My strong will has protected me from impetuous acts and impulsive decisions. My strong will has enabled me to look at life and relationships from a broad perspective.

—Rachel Yoder Bird

---

definitely preparing me for future ministry, but thankfully I did not have to participate in every lesson. I know and love a lot of former bad girls, and I don't know anyone who serves Christ with more passion and intensity. But believe it or not, not every bad girl is strong-willed, and not every strong-willed woman is a rebel.

Myth 4: Strong-Willed Women Can't Be Quiet or Compliant

The auditorium was full of frustrated parents who wanted strategies for dealing with strong-willed children. I asked the crowd three questions: "How many of you have your very own strong-willed child?" Virtually everyone raised a hand. "How many of you married a strong-willed child?" After a startled pause, at least a third of the audience raised a hand. "How many of you *are* a strong-willed child?" Over half of the group raised a hand.

After the seminar, one frustrated mother quickly approached me at the front of the room. "It's *me!*" she exclaimed. "*I'm* the strong-willed child, and I thought I was here for my daughter." She went on to explain that she had never thought of herself as strong willed because she had always been the quiet one in her family. She had not ever been loud or obnoxious or rude, and yet it was almost impossible to get her to change her mind once it was made up. If she encountered opposition, she simply went underground, quietly finding a way to achieve her goals without causing a fuss or drawing attention to the fact she wasn't following the rules.

Her daughter, on the other hand, was a much more openly strong-willed person, confronting any individual or situation that

In Her Own Words

There were several times when I just wanted to share something with someone, and because of my "ways," they think that I am criticizing them or condemning them.

—NINELIVES

placed restrictions on her free will. The mom smiled when she confessed that she had made a startling discovery. "You asked how many of us had a strong-willed child, and I raised my hand high," she said. "Then you asked how many of us married a strong-willed child, and I didn't raise my hand, because my husband really isn't. But when I looked at him, *his hand was in the air!* That's when I realized my daughter had come by it honestly."

Many of you reading this book are like me. I'm about as strong willed as they come, yet most of the trouble I cause often can't even be traced back to me! Outwardly, I'm relatively easy to get along with, cooperating and being a part of the team. But when you back me into a corner, point your bony finger in my face, and tell me to do it or else, that's when I'll just "else." I know there's nothing I really *have* to do, except die, which I'm willing to do. If I'm willing to die and you're not, I win. Okay, I'm dead, but I win.

Sometimes the battles are loud and obvious, but often they are grim and quiet. It's usually easier to identify and deal with a strong-willed person who is outspoken and confrontational than it is with those who may simply choose to slip into the background and drop off the radar screen as they go about the business of doing things their way.

Myth 5: Strong-Willed Women Can't Take Orders or Work for Someone

When people find out I worked as a police officer, they are surprised. The police department is a paramilitary organization; when you are told to do something by a superior officer, you can't argue or compromise. You don't call the shots or decide whether you want to obey an order. How could someone as strong willed as I am possibly survive in a system that is so autocratic? The answer is simple. I voluntarily surrendered to that authority. I knew going in what would be required of me, and I made the decision to do it. I *chose* to obey orders and be the best subordinate I could be. Of course, I quickly worked my way into a position of leadership, but I paid my dues along the way and followed established procedures in the process.

As a strong-willed individual, I will never let anyone take my will without my permission, but if I give it to you, you'll be surprised at how easy it is to get along with me. One of my

---

In Her Own Words

My strong will has, rightly and wrongly, been perceived by family, friends, peers, and coworkers as pride, stubbornness, selfishness, and arrogance. I have had to learn gentleness and diplomacy, so I am not forceful in my communication style. I've learned when persistence is not needed or wanted. I've learned to discern when my strong-willed behavior or words are hurting a situation or relationship, so I can modify my approach.

—RACHEL YODER BIRD

---

favorite passages in the gospel of John is in chapter 10, when Christ essentially says the same thing: "This is why the Father loves me: because I freely lay down my life. And so I am free to take it up again. No one takes it from me. I lay it down of my own free will. I have the right to lay it down; I also have the right to take it up again. I received this authority personally from my Father" (John 10:17–18).

God himself is the only one who could ever force anyone to do anything against his or her own free will. He never has, and he never will. There are certain immutable laws of the universe; there are inevitable consequences for wrongdoing. But God will never force us to serve him. The Christian strong-willed woman is most effective because she has surrendered her strong will to the one who placed it in her in the first place. We can be effective in any position, whether it's leadership or servanthood, when we have made a conscious choice to place ourselves under the authority of someone we trust. As long as we enlist, we can be an effective part of the team. If we're drafted against our wills, we're all in for trouble!

Let Me Help You Understand

Some of you may be thinking of someone right now who should be reading this chapter so he or she would understand you better. You're wondering why so many people misunderstand your strong-willed nature and often assume the worst in you. How will you make them see the error of their ways? You won't have to. As a strong-willed woman whose heart belongs to God, you'll be more concerned with keeping your life grounded in Jesus Christ than defending your actions and outlook. If

---

In Her Own Words

The combination of being strong willed and being a Christian is a grace-filled blessing! Other words for strong will, to me, are determination, tenacity, inner strength, faith.

—DCEALLAIGH

---

you're determined to use your strong will to bring honor and glory to God, you won't have time to worry about what others think, as long as your heart is right and your motives are pure.

The best way to help others understand why you do things the way you do is to try to understand their actions and intentions. Set the example, and you'll be surprised how effectively you'll destroy the negative preconceptions so many have about your strong will.

chapter 3

What's the Difference between Strong Willed and Compliant?

Since this is the kind of life we have chosen, the life of the Spirit, let us make sure that we do not just hold it as an idea in our heads or a sentiment in our hearts, but work out its implications in every detail of our lives. That means we will not compare ourselves with each other as if one of us were better and another worse. We have far more interesting things to do with our lives. Each of us is an original.

—Galatians 5:25–26

I was on one of my frequent shopping trips with my sister, Sandee. We'd been to a couple of stores I'd wanted to visit, so I asked her where *she* wanted to go. She shook her head. "It doesn't matter. I never try to buy anything for myself when I'm shopping with you," she said.

I couldn't believe it. What was she talking about?

She shrugged. "It's not worth it to me," she explained. "You already know where you want to go and what you want to do, and I'd feel too much pressure if I tried to get you to wait for me to do what I want."

I protested. After all, that makes me sound so *selfish*. But Sandee wouldn't even argue with me.

"It's fine," she assured me. "Let's just go where you want."

And just like that, she won. She won because she steadfastly refused to fight, and that's what has kept our relationship so healthy through the years.

If there were only two choices—strong willed or compliant—my sister would definitely come down on the compliant side, but she is anything but weak willed. I tell people it took my parents five years after they had me before they had the courage to try again. I was a stubborn, independent child, and it took all the time and energy they could muster to keep me on the straight and narrow path. My sister was a welcome change, with her sweet disposition and generally easygoing nature. She quickly learned what it took to get along well with everyone, and if she ever even needed punishment, a frown or disapproving look was all it took. I liked her from the beginning. She looked up to me, and she followed my lead without argument. I found out I could make endless deals with her, and she almost always went along with me.

What really intrigued me was the fact she didn't let me walk all over her. If she'd reached her limit with my deal making or she had decided she absolutely wasn't going to do what I asked, she simply walked away. She would not engage in verbal battles or try to defeat me on my terms. Neither of us realized at the time that she had discovered that this is one of the most effective ways to get along well with a strong-willed person.

Strong-willed women may have been misunderstood for a long time, but the fact is, we have seriously underestimated the worth of our counterparts as well. Since we've exploded a few myths about strong-willed women, let's get rid of a few about compliant women. If you look in the dictionary, you'll find that the verb *comply* comes from the Latin *complere* and the Spanish word *cumplir,* meaning "to complete." In *Webster's Unabridged Dictionary,* the definition says "to complement, to finish, to fulfill, to accomplish." That doesn't sound like a weak-willed doormat to me. It sounds like someone who provides a left hand to go with my right, a plan of action to go with my visionary idea. If you are a strong-willed woman and believe your opposite is someone who is timid, undecided, or subservient, think again.

Compliant Complements

Let me tell you why I count on compliant people to bring completion and fulfillment to my life, and why I truly enjoy being a part of theirs.

In Her Own Words

I learned to be strong willed in an effort to gain some control over my environment because everything was always so out of control at school and at home. Inside I was probably a marshmallow, but on the outside I was white knuckles all the way.

It has been refreshing to get older and be able to learn that I can lean fully on God; I can even lean on friends and my husband too without losing my position or strength. Does that make sense? I used to think if I ever let down my guard, I would either fall apart or be taken advantage of.

— SHARI RUSCH FURNSTAHL

Being Compliant Doesn't Mean Being a Pushover

As a strong-willed woman, I find it almost impossible to tolerate being with a person who is weak willed or indecisive. I can't respect someone who won't hold firm to personal convictions and moral standards. My compliant sister has certain issues she holds near and dear to her heart, and she just won't budge or compromise. I can be a very persuasive person, but the compliant friends and family members who mean the most to me simply won't let me talk them out of certain ideas, beliefs, and actions. To be honest, I do tend to get my way more often than anyone else does, but I've learned to respect the boundaries that are most important to those who live and work with me. Every strong-willed person I've talked to agrees that when we push, we expect that person to push back. If you display weakness in the form of a tentative, uncertain demeanor, in spite of our best efforts, we have to move in and take over.

Being Compliant Doesn't Mean Never Being Strong Willed

It was a few days before Christmas, and in addition to having the street in front of the house torn up, Sandee suddenly found every toilet in the house had backed up. Money was tight, yet she had no choice but to call a plumbing service. The serviceman they sent turned out to be very young and inexperienced. After spending almost two hours poking around and digging up different parts of the yard, he still couldn't figure out what the problem was—but he admitted it was getting worse. And oh, by the way, this service call was actually going to cost a bit more than the original estimate—about three times more. Even the most compliant woman has moments when her strong will kicks

---

In Her Own Words

My strong will finally had a voice after my daughter was hurt in a car accident. She suffered a traumatic brain injury. I had to become her advocate for the lengthy hospital and rehab stay. Prior to her accident, I always tried to please everyone. My background of a legalistic church taught me that a good Christian was one with a compliant nature and that a strong will was a bad thing. I realized very quickly that I didn't have time to worry about any of that anymore. I believe that I became more defined as a result of that experience.

My mom always knew me as a compliant person and couldn't believe this change in me! When I would stand up to her, she would say, "What has happened to you? What's the matter with you?" She still struggles with me being so strong willed. I work hard to be respectful and, at the same time, expect that respect from her or anyone else.

— YVONNE MUSTERMAN

---

in and she becomes a force to be reckoned with. Sandee pictured the money for her children's Christmas gifts being flushed down the toilet and decided she wasn't going to take it anymore. Her husband later described her as "a warrior" as he told how she lit into that poor kid with his hand out for payment. The bottom line? The young ineffective plumber left without a dime, and the construction company that tore up the street fixed the problem for free. Sandee may not have been born a strong-willed woman, but she can be *my* understudy any day!

Being Compliant Doesn't Mean You Never Argue

One of my favorite jokes is a story I heard several years ago about a woman whose husband was gravely ill. The doctor asked the husband to sit in the waiting room so he could speak privately with the wife.

"Your husband is very sick," the doctor explained, "and only you will be able to help him. You must never again argue with him. You must do whatever he wishes, never disagree with him, and make sure he has everything he wants. If you don't do this, he will die. Do you understand?"

The woman nodded solemnly and went to join her husband in the waiting room. Her husband stood and asked anxiously, "Honey? What did the doctor say?"

She looked at him sadly. "I'm sorry, dear, but he says you're going to die."

Even the most compliant woman couldn't fill that prescription!

Healthy disagreements are a natural part of any relationship. However, the compliant woman doesn't seem to struggle as much as the strong-willed woman with deciding what's worth arguing about and what should be overlooked. There's no real "killer instinct" when drawing the battle lines, and it's frequently the compliant friend of a strong-willed woman who can soften attitudes and diffuse confrontations. One of the things I appreciate most about my compliant counterparts is their refusal to argue on my strong-willed, all-or-nothing, take-no-prisoners terms. They take no pleasure in verbal duels and don't mind backing down and walking away when they see no positive results coming from the situation.

Three Primary Differences

If I were to sum up the major differences between the compliant woman and the strong-willed woman, three major areas come to mind.

Risk Taking

My sister has told me several times she considers me the trailblazer and herself the trail walker. My strong-willed nature encourages me to go out on a limb at a moment's notice, even if I'm not sure it will bear my weight. My compliant sister stands ready to join me if it works or to administer first aid if it doesn't. She assures me she's thankful for the trailblazers, but if there weren't trail walkers, there'd just be lots of empty paths.

Teamwork

When I was working with my Strong-Willed Women for Christ focus group, I asked them the question, "Can a strong-willed woman be a team player?" The response was instantaneous and unanimous: Of course—as long as *we* choose the team! Many of us even admit to the truth of a slogan I saw on a T-shirt recently: "Teamwork is everyone doing it my way." As a rule, it's the more compliant woman who can work in harmony with almost anyone. That's just another reason to appreciate how the partnership between strong-willed and compliant women can bring out the best in both.

Patience

I readily admit I am probably the least patient person in my family. As I have matured, I think I've gotten better, but my strong-willed nature keeps me constantly looking for ways I can move things along. I often admire my compliant sister's willingness to bide her time or delay action. If nothing's happening, I want to *do* something, anything to move it along! It is my compliant friends and colleagues who help me take a deep breath, sit tight, and think twice before I jump off that cliff!

Is It Better to Be Strong Willed or Compliant?

It should be pretty obvious by now that there are definite advantages to being either strong willed or compliant. Rather than being at odds with each other, we can actually make an incredibly effective team. Perhaps the key lies in not being defensive about who we are but being appreciative of what we can do together. Instead of the strong-willed woman pushing her compliant counterparts into uncomfortable territory, she can seek ways to garner their support for her new ideas. Rather than resent the sometimes brash and impatient methods used by strong-willed women, their compliant partners can cheer them on, thankful that someone is willing to go first.

The bottom line is that the world certainly needs both of us. God, in his infinite wisdom, has provided a way to achieve the kind of balance that keeps the world on track!

In Her Own Words

One thing I've learned: be prepared to be singled out as the object of the stereotypical strong-willed-woman joke at the annual Christmas party. Ah well, the laugh's on all of us because a merry heart does good like a medicine.

— ANONYMOUS

A Revolutionary Idea

I have long thought that most women's ministry programs and events were geared more to compliant women than to those of us who are strong willed. I have to admit that although I occasionally attend, I most often avoid these women's gatherings. Maybe it's just me, but the pace seems too slow, the focus too gentle, and the speaking too soft. Don't get me wrong; there are some incredibly effective women's groups. If you think about it, most compliant women would avoid attending high-powered, strong-willed events if that was the only emphasis. Wait a minute—I can't *think* of any strong-willed women events!

Isn't it time that Christian women come together—both compliant and strong willed—and try to figure out how to make this teamwork an unstoppable force for the kingdom of God? Our goal would not be to change one another to the way *we* believe a Christian woman should look and act. Our focus would be to allow God to work according to his original design, bringing a myriad of beautiful strong-willed and compliant hearts to the same banquet table, where the guest of honor is Jesus Christ.

part 2

The Strong-Willed Woman and Her Relationships

chapter 4

Strong-Willed Women on Their Own

Sometimes I wish everyone were single like me—a simpler life in many ways! But celibacy is not for everyone any more than marriage is. God gives the gift of the single life to some, the gift of the married life to others.

—1 Corinthians 7:7

In the beginning, I had no idea attending a Christian singles function could be so scary. After all, I was twenty-five years old, a career woman full of confidence and capable in diverse job skills. I never dreamed that walking into a room filled with other single people could make me break out into a cold sweat. The friend who had talked me into this whole thing was beside me, and I heard her inhale sharply when we stepped into the room. All eyes had turned to us. My mind raced with first impressions. Instantly I noticed that all the women were on one side of the room and all the men were on the other. As much as I try not to judge by appearance, I couldn't help noticing that no one else looked like my picture of a young professional or a happy, well-adjusted independent adult. Over the next hour or so, my friend and I moved uncomfortably around the room, stiffly acknowledging people who introduced themselves to us.

It didn't take long to figure out I didn't have much in common with this particular group of singles. They seemed so eager to find someone to marry, so unhappy to be living alone. It honestly hadn't occurred to me to resent the fact I wasn't married. If anything, I was thrilled to be independent and free to pursue a variety of jobs and hobbies while I wasn't tied to family obligations. But I was definitely in the minority among this Christian singles group.

My friend and I excused ourselves early and promised each other we would never try anything that foolish again. "What's wrong with being single?" we asked each other. We weren't in search of a husband; we were looking for friendships with men *and* women who shared common interests and goals. I was never desperate to be married, even though I certainly wasn't opposed to it if I found the right guy.

Many single strong-willed women find themselves being pressured by well-meaning family and friends when there appears to be no prospective husband on the horizon, especially once they're over the age of twenty-five. I was so blessed to have parents who didn't bother me at all about waiting to get married until I was in my thirties. I honestly believe they would be just as happy with my life and success if I had never married at

---

In Her Own Words

As a single, strong-willed woman, I am proud to be picky—it is one of my strongest assets. Life is fantastic and fun!

—JOYCIE YEE

---

all (although they love my husband and children!). Unfortunately, some of my friends didn't keep as low a profile as my family; by the time I hit thirty, I'd heard a lot of warnings and criticisms about not being married.

Deflecting the Arrows

Just in case you happen to be in that situation right now, let me give you a few suggestions for defending yourself against these often ridiculous statements. If you are a well-meaning family member or friend of a single woman, please take heed!

You're Too Picky

"You're just too picky! You're never going to find the perfect man! Your standards are too high!" These and other similar statements have to make you wonder how many of your friends may have lowered their standards to get a husband. Surely if they really thought about what they were saying, they would realize no one should simply "settle" for someone who isn't the right fit.

A friend of mine was really feeling the pressure to be married and had decided it was better to go ahead and at least settle down with a man she liked and had been friends with for years. How big a deal was it to be "in love" anyway? Having been married for a few years by then myself, I was quick to assure her it was more important than she thought. Marriage is a difficult day-to-day challenge even when you are passionately in love with someone. I can't imagine how you would survive if you weren't really in love! Too picky? I'd encourage that any day over the alternative!

Biological Clock

"You're going to be past your child-bearing years!" First of all, we have some pretty wonderful technology these days, and to be considered an "older mother," you usually have to be significantly past your fortieth birthday. The age-old adage of listening to your biological clock should not be used as ammunition against you; getting married just to beat the clock is a terrible idea anyway. I was thirty-seven when our twins were born, and we were blessed not to have needed fertility treatments. But we discussed the possibilities at length before I got pregnant. There are so many options these days when it comes to being a parent, including fertility procedures and adoption. I have several friends who married late and are quite content to have no children. They stay involved with other people's children, including relatives and church ministries, but they are not dissatisfied with God for "cheating" them out of their own children. Some couples may never have children, and if we truly believe that God is in control, we dare not doubt his wisdom and timing.

You're Too Busy

"You're staying too busy to ever find a husband!" I've never quite understood this criticism, although for years I heard it from some of my friends. What was I supposed to do, just sit at home by the phone and hope my dream guy would call? My strong-willed nature contributes to my naturally varied and active lifestyle, and I could never imagine leaving big gaps in my schedule on the off chance I'd get a date. I believe that staying busy will, if anything, help you find someone who shares your interests and understands your drive to succeed. Although it may not be true for every strong-willed woman, I found that whenever I started to feel stress or discouragement, I simply took on another project to keep my mind off what was bothering me. The bottom line is that most of us are going to stay busy anyway. If your ideal man appears, I don't think you'll be too busy to notice.

You'll Intimidate Him

"Don't be so intimidating; you're scaring men away!" Just about every strong-willed woman has to face this accusation at some point. It seems that if you appear too self-sufficient, men will think you don't need them or will feel threatened by your strength and independence. Having had my heart broken by a man who claimed he found someone who needed him more than I ever would, I can relate to this, but I can tell you that it didn't take me long to figure out that he was definitely the

----

In Her Own Words

I speak my mind. I don't like to play games or act like something is other than what it is. I guess I rock the boat.

Because I tend to be more vocal, often I am judged as pushy or bossy when I'm just making suggestions or offering an opinion. This happens even when I carefully word something so it's not offensive. The fact that I'm even (as a woman) speaking out about something or stating that I'm knowledgeable about something puts some people off ... usually people who are less secure in their abilities or knowledge.

—ANONYMOUS

----

wrong man for me. I'm not about to play the helpless female to attract a man who just wants to feel needed. On the other hand, I'm not invulnerable; I enjoy being in a relationship in which I am loved and appreciated. Although I know I need to be careful about being too bossy or critical, if knowing my own mind and standing up for my convictions makes me intimidating, so be it. As I can personally attest, the right man won't be put off by the honesty and confidence of a strong-willed woman who has dedicated her heart to the one who made her who she is in the first place.

There's Someone for Everyone

"There's someone for everyone." This statement always struck fear into my heart, because it's usually followed with examples of abnormal or socially unacceptable women who were still able to find a true love, no matter how weird or unlikely the pairing seemed. Is that how my friends were starting to perceive me? Does everyone have a soul mate just waiting to be discovered? Maybe in the movies, but you'll never convince me that women who never marry just didn't try hard enough. There *is* someone for everyone, but he is Jesus Christ, and he's perfect for every single woman in the world. His grace is sufficient, and he will never leave us feeling unloved or unwanted.

One strong-willed woman usually answers the question "When are you getting married?" with, "I haven't had an offer I couldn't refuse." It always brought a laugh and kept people from asking a second question.[1] As you find yourself having to defend yourself to those who wonder why you're not married, remember not to protest too much. The more you have to con-

In Her Own Words

The key is to remember whom I belong to—Christ. My will can bend more easily to him than to anyone (or anything) else. This is because he is who he is. And he loves me.

—ANONYMOUS

vince someone you're happy to be unmarried, the more likely it is that you're kidding yourself. When the subject comes up, stay calm and cheerful and talk about something else. It will drive them crazy!

Love through Another Route

I know there are many single women who struggle to understand why they haven't found the right man. Others get very defensive about their choice to be unmarried. And still others are calmly content with their singleness. The key lies in whether they have simply resigned themselves or have accepted their singleness joyfully, confident of God's love and purpose for their lives.

One of the most significant and wonderful books I have ever read is Catherine Marshall's classic *Beyond Ourselves,* in which she describes the difference between creative acceptance and sterile resignation.

Resignation is barren of faith in the love of God. It says, "Grievous circumstances have come to me. There is no escaping them. I am only one creature, an alien in a vast unknowable creation. I have no heart left even to rebel. So I'll just resign myself to what apparently is the will of God; I'll even try to make a virtue out of patient submission." So resignation lies down quietly in the dust of a universe from which God seems to have fled, and the door of Hope swings shut.

But turn the coin over. Acceptance says, "I trust the good will, the love of my God. I'll open my arms and my understanding to what He has allowed to come to me. Since I know that He means to make all things work together for good, I consent to this present situation with hope for what the future will bring." Thus acceptance leaves the door of Hope wide open to God's creative plan.[2]

Catherine uses the term "prayer of relinquishment" to describe a turning point—giving up control to God. I remember reaching a point where I decided it was okay if God never provided a husband and children for me. I won't tell you it was an easy decision, but I honestly sensed that I could accept whatever God ordained for my life.

I think of a dramatic turning point in the life of Corrie ten Boom. There's a timeless message for strong-willed singles in her autobiography, *The Hiding Place,* though you might not think so from reading the marketing teaser on the cover of a 1974 Bantam Books edition. It describes this "heroine of the anti-Nazi underground" as a "50-year-old spinster." Ouch. A line like that would never work today. In *The Hiding Place* she describes the great love—and heartbreak—of her life.

In her twenties she fell in love with a young man named Karel. On long walks they talked of their future together, though no one ever said the word *marriage.* He went off to the university; they corresponded; but then one day she opened the front door to find him standing there with another woman. He wanted Corrie to meet his fiancée. With understatement Corrie writes, "Somehow the half-hour passed. Somehow I managed to shake her hand, then Karel's hand, and to wish them every happiness."

As soon as they were out the door, she ran to her bedroom, where her father later found her. As you might understand, strong-willed Corrie didn't want to hear lies from him. "Suddenly I was afraid of what Father would say. Afraid he would say, 'There'll be someone else soon,' and that forever afterward this untruth would lie between us. For in some deep part of me I knew already that there would not—soon or ever—be anyone else."

Corrie's wise father did not give idle promises. He talked about love, the pain one feels when it is blocked, and the two ways people react to the pain.

> "We can kill the love so that it stops hurting. But then of course part of us dies, too. Or, Corrie, we can ask God to open up another route for that love to travel.
>
> "God loves Karel—even more than you do—and if you ask Him, He will give you His love for this man, a love nothing can prevent, nothing destroy. Whenever we cannot love in the old, human way, Corrie, God can give us the perfect way."

Corrie continues,

> I did not know . . . that he had given me more than the key to this hard moment. . . . He had put into my hands the secret that would open far darker rooms than this—places where there was not, on a human level, anything to love at all. . . . My task just then was to give up my feeling for Karel without giving up the joy and wonder that had grown with it. And so, that very hour, lying there on my bed, I whispered the enormous prayer:

"Lord, I give to You the way I feel about Karel, my thoughts about our future—oh, You know! Everything! Give me Your way of seeing Karel instead. Help me to love him that way. That much."[3]

With the help of her father's advice, Corrie did not kill the pain of denied love but willingly used the energy of that love to change the landscape of her world—not out of resignation but for and with joy and wonder.

Positive Option

I had prayed the Prayer of Relinquishment. I wasn't feeling cheated that I couldn't be married, but I didn't feel clearly called to be single forever, either. I didn't want to just accept the situation without at least checking out the options. As I mentioned at the beginning of the chapter, at the very least, I wanted to broaden my base of friendships with other single men and women. If church-based singles groups weren't going to yield any results, where could I go? I was working for an attorney in downtown Seattle at this point, finishing my master's degree in learning styles and working the streets in my police uniform on the weekends. I probably *was* too busy to make room for dating, but until I found someone worth taking time off for, I wasn't inclined to change my schedule.

I read an article in a women's magazine that touted the idea of putting in a classified ad to find the man of your dreams. At first I dismissed the concept as ridiculous, but the more I thought about it, the more it intrigued me. What if I just gave it a shot? I wouldn't put the ad in just *any* paper. I did a little research by observing what newspaper the professional men around me seemed to be reading. It was an upscale, urban newspaper that had a very creative "Person to Person" section. After more thought and more than a little writing and rewriting, I placed an ad—just for fun. Here's what it said: "Attractive, professional female, thirty-one, seeks a man committed to the solid values in life. If you're looking for casual sex, you're not looking for me; if you want a friendship, let's explore the possibilities."

In response I received twenty-one letters right away, and I met nine of the letter writers. I was very careful to meet in a public place and not share any personal information while my host was a stranger. I also trusted my instincts—I always have—and all the men I met turned out to be professional in manner and pleasant in disposition. I did make some new friends, and one of those friends asked me to marry him a year later. At the age of thirty-three, I turned in my single life for a marriage well worth waiting for.

If you want to explore your options, I would encourage you to do your searching for the right reasons. Pray about it and ask God to direct your paths. Remember men can smell desperation from a great distance, and that tends to ruin your chances for a nonthreatening friendship.

If you feel clear about wanting marriage, decide where you'd like to look for possible relationships. Besides the classified ads (which obviously don't work out the same for everyone as they did for me!), there are organizations and publications that can offer you a safe and faith-based database of men who may well share your beliefs and interests. In the end, the solution will likely be as unique as the problem, and only you can decide what's best.

Serving God While Single

A strong-willed single woman, committed to God and his kingdom work, has a great opportunity to make a difference in her world.

As a single woman, you are often in a unique and wonderful position to invest a significant part of your life in places where you can really make a difference. You have more flexibility and options, more opportunities to just pick up and follow a new challenge. Whether it's a foreign mission field, an inner-city ministry, or a temporary work and witness project, you can take advantage of the fact that you need to support only yourself, and that usually means you can get by with less money and put up with more inconvenience than your married counterparts. What a unique and wonderful position a single strong-willed woman can find herself in when she simply makes herself available to the first true love in her life—Jesus Christ! I personally found it immensely rewarding to be able to spend so much time doing the Master's work during the years there was no one home to really miss me.

Whether you will stay permanently single or eventually get married, the only thing that really matters is your relationship with God, and no one else can control that for you.

chapter 5

Strong-Willed Women and the Men Who Love Them

It is absolutely clear that God has called you to a free life. Just make sure that you don't use this freedom as an excuse to do whatever you want to do and destroy your freedom. Rather, use your freedom to serve one another in love; that's how freedom grows. For everything we know about God's Word is summed up in a single sentence: Love others as you love yourself. That's an act of true freedom.

—Galatians 5:13–14

At one of my recent seminars, I mentioned I had picked up a copy of the book *The Surrendered Wife* by Laura Doyle. One woman blurted out what several must have been thinking: "Did you find it in the science fiction section?" Fortunately, my husband was smiling! I have to admit, I don't think anyone who knows a strong-willed woman would think of her in terms of a "surrendered wife." Perhaps it's because the word *surrender* has such a negative connotation. To us it means admitting defeat, turning tail and running, giving up all control.

Although I find the title of the book highly offensive and I disagree with most of the content, I did read enough of it to realize that the author does not define her terms the same way I do. She urges the surrendered wife to relinquish inappropriate control of her husband and to respect his thinking. I can go along with that. She ends up defining "the surrendered wife" as someone who will "stop trying to control everything." Okay, I admit it; I do like to control things. But I don't even want to control *everything,* especially when it comes to my marriage. I wouldn't have much respect for my husband if he just gave in all the time. But I also wouldn't respect him if he always had to be in charge. One of the things I like best about him is that he is willing to share control without simply letting me take over. But there's no doubt that the whole institution of marriage presents one of the greatest challenges of all for strong-willed women everywhere. There are thousands of books about marriage, and I'll recommend some of my favorites at the end of this book. There are some basic tenets that make a marriage healthy regardless of strong will or compliance, and we certainly don't have the time or the need to go over the whole thing here. So let's just take a quick, hard look at why being a happily married strong-willed woman has some unique aspects.

What Kind of Men Are Strong-Willed Women Usually Drawn To?

There are, of course, as many different varieties of men that strong-willed women marry as there are women themselves. But there are, I believe, at least five characteristics that a strong-willed woman's husband should ideally possess to lay the groundwork for a successful Christian marriage.

He Is a Godly Man

This, above all else, is the stone that helps hold the others in place, even in times of hardship or incompatibility. The man who has genuinely dedicated his life to Jesus Christ will always support a solid foundation for a godly marriage. A marriage can be doomed from the beginning without God directly in the center of the relationship.

He Is Comfortable with Himself

Everyone in my Strong-Willed Women focus group, regardless of marital status, immediately mentioned this as an important trait. We struggle to get along with any man who seems unsure of himself or talks wistfully about who he wishes he could be. We love it when a man seems to be at ease with who and what he is, regardless of his physical or occupational attributes.

He Is Confident in His Abilities

Strong-willed women seek out those who exhibit confidence and strength. This doesn't mean we're just looking for a superhero or a muscle man; it means the man we love is not tentative or weak in his approach to life and work. He understands his strengths and limitations and focuses on what he knows he can do.

He Is Not Threatened or Intimidated by Strong-Willed Women

It was a wonderful discovery for me to find out how many men actually search out strong-willed women. Far from being intimidated, they are challenged and refreshed by the sharpening of "steel against steel." I knew I had found my match when John took me out on a date even while I was wearing a full police uniform and packing a .357 Magnum on my waist!

He Steadfastly Offers Me Unconditional Love

As strong-willed women, we often have a hard time imagining that someone could always love us, regardless of how unlovable we sometimes are. There is, deep in our hearts, a desire to know that our husbands will not quit and walk away just because we had a terrible argument. We need to know we are both in this for the long haul, no matter how hard things may get.

Hazards for the Strong-Willed Wife

Most strong-willed women will fight passionately to keep their marriage together, if for no other reason than we hate thinking of ourselves as quitters. There are, of course, some drastic causes for failed marriages (abuse, etc.). Aside from those, however, there are some especially treacherous hazards even for the strong-willed wife in a perfectly healthy relationship.

In Her Own Words

I probably would have had an affair and/or been divorced if it weren't for my trust in God, as well as the fact that I am too stubborn to go back on my vows once I've made them! I would absolutely hate to do what everyone else seems to be doing (i.e., more than 50 percent of marriages break up; an estimated 70 percent of people have affairs). I am also so concrete that if the Bible says, "Thou shalt not commit adultery," then I just don't, plain and simple.

—Anonymous

Who's in Charge?

The strong-willed woman who has dedicated her life to Christ does not live at cross purposes with God's Word by demanding her rights. On the contrary, all the women in my focus group quickly agreed that God's plan for women with respect to their husbands' leadership as outlined in Ephesians 5:22–23 is not something we are seeking to overturn:

> Out of respect for Christ, be courteously reverent to one another.
>
> Wives, understand and support your husbands in ways that show your support for Christ. The husband provides leadership to his wife the way Christ does to his church, not by domineering but by cherishing. So just as the church submits to Christ as he exercises such leadership, wives should likewise submit to their husbands.
>
> Husbands, go all out in your love for your wives, exactly as Christ did for the church—a love marked by giving, not getting. Christ's love makes the church whole. . . . Everything he does and says is designed to bring the best out in her. . . . And that is how husbands ought to love their wives. They're really doing themselves a favor—since they're already "one" in marriage.

When it comes to the roles of husband and wife, the term *submit* has never meant "be subjugated." Men cannot justify domination or abuse in the name of submission. By the same token, women cannot justify "equal rights" based on their resentment of God's designation of the husband as the leader of the household. With Christ as the center of our marriage, we both seek to love and serve one another, not to compete for status or rank.

In Her Own Words

As a strong-willed woman, I am often tagged or joked about as being "unsubmissive" in general and in particular to my husband. My husband, who has a compliant, easygoing nature, is also tagged as the victim of the strong-willed, unsubmissive wife. I am very vocal about issues in our lives and have at times acted independently of my husband. This has gotten me in trouble particularly in the area of finances; I should have saved when instead I spent.

I lived and learned the lesson of bringing that independent will into check and accountability, no pun intended. But in general, I think the secret delight of being a strong-willed woman in a marriage relationship is this: when she will first submit to the authority and deity of Christ, she then has the freedom to willingly submit to the leadership role God has given her husband, regardless of his personality style. It is also always very helpful when that husband is submitted to the authority of Jesus Christ in his life and in the marriage.

—ANONYMOUS

The challenge for strong-willed women comes when we find ourselves being a little too bossy, demanding too much, or having a critical spirit. It comes so naturally for us! It doesn't mean we're trying to take over, but it can sure create some serious obstacles to a mutually loving and respectful relationship.

Whose Stuff Is This?

One of the hardest parts of marriage for me may seem a little silly to some people. I have a naturally territorial nature, and

I just about come unglued if my husband starts messing with my stuff. Now I don't have a problem with changing my name, sharing a joint checking account, or pooling our financial resources. But it just drives me crazy when he starts reorganizing my closet or cleaning off my dresser when I'm not home. After talking to dozens of other strong-willed wives, I found out I'm not alone! There is a certain personal parking space in our lives that is reserved only for those who have permission to be there, and even then it is loading and unloading only. If you park without permission, you'll be towed away, and it's expensive to retrieve your vehicle and make things right again. Sometimes I feel a bit guilty, but I really need that personal distance when it comes to my cherished possessions, no matter how ridiculous and unimportant they seem to my husband.

I can't blame John for trying to organize my things in a way that makes sense to him, because it's certainly a natural tendency in almost everyone. But I *am* working on more positive ways to let him know what's important to me and what will keep peace and harmony between us. His sudden urges to reorganize and redistribute my clutter are becoming fewer and farther between, and my instant anger at what I perceive as his intrusion into my privacy is not as frequent or intense as it used to be.

Who's Sorry Now?

In my first book, *The Way They Learn,* I told a story that has now become the classic illustration for the difference between how my husband apologizes and how I say I'm sorry. It has always been very difficult for me to apologize, even though I will definitely make things right when I realize I am wrong. The actual words "I'm sorry" are infrequent visitors to my lips, even when my heart seeks to make amends. Early in our courtship, John and I had a very heated argument and I realized he was right. I took a deep breath and actually did bring myself to say those foreign words: "John, I'm sorry." He nodded but replied, "Well, Cindy, 'sorry' is a statement of condition; 'apologize' is the active verb. Now are you sorry, or do you apologize?" You guessed it—*neither* at that point! It was hours before I even *spoke* to him again!

It has been a sore spot in our marriage from the beginning. John feels he apologizes at least ten times more often than I do. That could be, since my apologies don't sound anything at all like his. I'm practicing, and I'm really trying to get better at saying the words that are important to him. I'm actually able to occasionally say to him, "I'm sorry—you were right." I still have a long way to go before I can add those other three important words: "I was wrong," but I'll keep working on it!

In Her Own Words

The hardest lesson that God has taught me is: "strong will" does not equal "overkill." God allowed my husband to teach me that! My "control freak" nature made me think that if I could just pound "my way" into his head and heart, he would finally see the light. Well, my strong-willed sisters in Christ, I had a lot to learn. After a near divorce and through lots of prayer, I learned that I must work daily at unconditional love, the kind that Jesus offers to us! What a relief it is to know that I do not have to be right all the time!

—JEAN CANADY

Preventing Nuclear Battles

Early in our marriage, John asked me the same question hundreds of people have asked me since: When the strong-willed woman is in the middle of a confrontation headed for meltdown, what can be done to stop the destruction? I've given it a lot of thought, asked a lot of strong-willed friends and acquaintances, and lived through enough of my own meltdowns to know how they work. But here's the thing: once the confrontation has begun, it's just like the president pushing the buttons that release the nuclear warheads; there's no turning back. I have told myself, in the middle of a heated argument with my husband, I should just back off of this. And I watch myself go down in flames, knowing full well what I could have done or said to prevent it. I don't think it's hopeless. I have compared notes with enough strong-willed women like me to know that there are two or three strategies that might just freeze that button before it is depressed. First of all, let's take a quick look at a few things that will almost always push that button. Husbands, take note— these are fighting words!

It almost always starts a nuclear battle if you say to a strong-willed woman:

- "Don't be so sensitive!"
- "What's your problem?"
- "You've got a bad attitude."
- "It must be nice to know it all."
- Anything with "why" and "you" in the same statement.

Okay. So you blew it and the fight is on. Before everyone is destroyed, the determined husband can try these midbattle strategies to silence the weapons:

- Put your arms around me and just remind me how much you love me and how glad you are you married me. (It may not work for everyone because it's bound to make your strong-willed wife even madder at first, but she can't argue with what you're saying, so give it a shot!)
- Back away and leave me alone for a while, but not too long. Leave me a note—friendly, affectionate; give me some space and wait for me to respond to you.

Maybe you can think of another strategy that would work best for you. I like the idea one strong-willed woman shared with me at a recent seminar. She said if her husband says something that really makes her mad, she looks right at him and declares, "I'm going to pretend you didn't just say that." Then she walks away. Don't try to come up with your strategy during the argument itself; try discussing it calmly at a time when you're not angry. I'm absolutely committed to my marriage, so it's worth the time and effort it will take for my husband and me to learn how to fight fair and make up quickly. If I truly want my strong will to bring honor and glory to God, I must learn to put myself aside and keep my husband first. Wow—that's harder than it sounds! I love this illustration from *On This Day* by Carl D. Windsor:

> Even the most devoted couple will experience a "stormy" bout once in awhile. A grandmother, celebrating her golden wedding anniversary, once told the secret of her long and happy marriage. "On my wedding day, I decided to make a list of ten of my husband's faults which, for the sake of our marriage, I would overlook," she said. A guest asked the woman what some of the faults she had chosen to over-

look were. The grandmother replied, "To tell you the truth, my dear, I never did get around to listing them. But whenever my husband did something that made me hopping mad, I would say to myself, *Lucky for him that's one of the ten!*"[1]

Awareness is at least half the battle. If I can recognize what I am doing and how it is affecting my husband, I can decide to improve. One of the promises we have made to each other is that we will never annoy one another on purpose. Of course, we're still bound to irritate each other, often daily, but you'd be surprised what a difference it makes when we know it's not deliberate!

Can He Love Me, Strong Will and All?

One of the things I love most about my husband is that he truly does appreciate me for who I am, even if it does make his life a lot more difficult at times! Just for fun, I recently decided to try out some of the tactics of the surrendered and submissive wife that several women's books insist will make marriage happier.

John asked me about something, and I replied, "Whatever you think is best, hon; that's fine with me."

A little later, he asked my opinion about a political issue, and I smiled sweetly and said, "I think *your* ideas are best."

He frowned at me and said, "You're creeping me out; what's the matter with you?"

I told him I was just trying to be more submissive, and he rolled his eyes. "Well cut it out!" he exclaimed. "I like you better as yourself."

Now that I know that, I can be nicer to him without feeling like I have to become a completely different person, and he knows he can count on having me speak my mind!

In Her Own Words

My husband loves me dearly, but quite honestly, I do drive him crazy. He is very easygoing and introverted. I, on the other hand, am very passionate and extroverted. I love being involved in ministry, leading and helping others discover their gifts. I sometimes feel that my husband should communicate with others, myself, and even God in the same way I do.

He admitted that at times I overwhelm him, yet he validates the effectiveness of my gifts and passions for ministry. I tried to listen and understand for the first time that his style really is different than mine and to love him for his relaxed, laid-back outlook on life and ministry. I am learning how important it is to love and respect my wonderful husband, who is completely my opposite. I have a long way to go!

—RCMONSON

Living with a Strong-Willed Woman

Although I don't give my husband equal time at conferences or seminars, and I've never had him write in any of my books, I thought this might be the right opportunity to let my readers get a glimpse of who John is and why he fits the bill for this strong-willed woman. I asked him to read this chapter up to here and then give a few brief comments. He wrote several paragraphs, but I've done a bit of editing! I can't help but think he speaks for many other husbands out there, so I'm actually going to let him have the last word—this time!

Having read the first part of this chapter at my wife's request, I feel equipped to give an observation or two regarding what she writes. So here goes.

First things first. You have to understand that my view of my wife is summed up in a shirt she gave me a few Christmases ago at my request. It depicts a bull standing next to a calf. Both are looking up in the sky at a cow jumping over the moon. The bull says to the calf, "You know, son, your mother really *is* a remarkable woman!" That happens to be how I view my wife. She is, in my judgment, pretty remarkable. For my part, I have probably always been drawn to women with a mind of their own. Girlfriends in high school and college were seldom cut of the cloth of the demure distaff gender. In my adult life, I found women who didn't go with the flow immeasurably more appealing than those who were swept along with some kind of great female tide. In short, I wanted the woman I married to have convictions of steel. What I got, of course, was kryptonite!

When she did her imitation of the surrendered wife, I admit it scared me more than just a little. I had to wonder, "Who *is* this person, and what has she done with my wife?"

Now before anyone goes thinking that I'm some kind of special, it is important that you know I'm a pretty average guy. While I may not be a saint according to my wife's five-point list, I admit I'm comfortable with myself and confident in my abilities. Would I be a better husband/person if I could? Of course, and I never stop trying. I'm obviously not threatened by my wife or her strength of will. And I love my God and my family. Sometimes, dealing with a strong-willed woman can be a challenge. But the secret, as Arthur sings in a song called "How to Handle a Woman" in *Camelot,* is "to love her . . . simply love her . . . merely love her . . . love her . . . love her."

In fifteen years of marriage, I've learned a few things. First, don't offer even constructive criticism (unless it involves saving life or limb) unless your opinion is specifically requested by the strong-willed woman in your life. You may like a little Parmesan sprinkled on your pizza as it's cooking. If she makes the pizza and forgets the Parmesan, forget it, or sprinkle your own cheese and put it under the broiler yourself. Do not—I repeat, do not—say something like, "Next time, would you please sprinkle a little Parmesan on mine?" lest you find yourself making your own pizza from now until your final day on this mortal soil. Appreciate the gesture she's made.

Can you love your strong-willed woman, strong will and all? For heaven's sake, it was her strong will that attracted you to her in the first place. Affirm her in it. Let her know that it is what makes her stand out. I "cut my teeth" on strong-willed women. Could I ever settle for anything less now?

chapter 6

Strong-Willed Moms Who Got the Kids They Deserved

Summing up: Be agreeable, be sympathetic, be loving, be compassionate, be humble. That goes for all of you, no exceptions. No retaliation. No sharp-tongued sarcasm. Instead, bless—that's your job, to bless. You'll be a blessing and also get a blessing.

—1 Peter 3:8–9

Our twin boys were only two years old when I made a rather disturbing discovery. I was always on the move, so the guys were quite accustomed to riding in their car seats in the back of our van. I bragged to John that I was a much better driver for having the boys in the car, because in their presence I didn't feel as free to express my feelings out loud about others on the road.

He nodded and said he was proud of me. A couple of days later, the boys and I were riding with John in his car. As we turned a corner, he accidentally honked his horn. Like an automatic response, two loud cheerful voices came from the car seats in the back: "C'mon, lady!" I grinned sheepishly. Come to think of it, I guess I do say that a lot!

It didn't take me long as a mom to figure out that my children take a lot of cues from me. It isn't just that they parrot my words and phrases; they do an amazingly accurate imitation of my tone of voice and nonverbal mannerisms.

I also discovered a much more disconcerting truth about myself as a parent: I often find myself saying things to my strong-willed child that I never would have responded to positively if I were in his place. In other words, as a strong-willed parent, I can dish it out, but I can't take it! Here I am making these sweeping authoritarian statements and handing down absolutely inflexible rules, all the while forgetting that those were the very things I resented most as a child.

Think about it for a moment; what bothered you most about your parents when you were a kid? What drove you crazy about school? What was the quickest way to make you mad? The chances are good that your answers will also be true

---

In Her Own Words

The strong-willed, hard-to-live-with part comes out most at home with my family. Over the years I've realized I must be hard to live with. I force my family to deal with my "high energy" and whatnot. I've learned lately that there's a season for everything and I can't possibly have it all in the same season. So I've focused the last several years on being there for my family and pouring some of that energy into them instead of everyone (everything) else. It's paying off!

—ANONYMOUS

---

for one or more of the children God so graciously gave you. I usually tell my audiences that I have a child who is very strong willed—Michael—because my mother prayed it would be so. Though "what goes around comes around" sounds good (and maybe she secretly wished it upon me), the truth is, God gave Michael to me as a compliment, not as pay-back. I understand Michael better than anyone else does. After all, who knows a strong-willed person better than another strong-willed person?

The trouble is that when we strong-willed moms lock horns with a child who has an equally strong will, neither of us wants to give and both of us are willing to fight to the death, so to speak. This presents a unique and compelling challenge to the strong-willed parent, and I'm sure I don't have to tell you how many difficult situations we can get ourselves into when the confrontations begin.

It doesn't have to be that way! We can hold on to our own strong will and parental authority without destroying our high-spirited offspring. In the course of writing my book *You Can't Make Me! (But I Can Be Persuaded),* I talked to hundreds of strong-willed children of all ages. I was surprised to discover some of the basic truths that virtually every one of them agreed upon, regardless of how rebellious they were or how distant they were from their parents' standards or values.

There are at least two critical elements that emerged in my discussions with these strong-willed kids when it comes to being at their best with their parents. As I share these with you, try to place yourself in your children's shoes while you remember what you were like as a child. Remember, when it comes to the strong-willed child, it takes one to know one!

Critical Element 1: Relationship

The relationship you cultivate and maintain with your child is more important than anything else. From the time our boys were babies, we have made it a point to cuddle with them first thing in the morning and last thing at night. These are special moments of conversation, affection, and reassurance. Mike, despite his strong will and stubborn nature, has always counted on spending this time of bonding with Mom and Dad. When Mike was only four or so, he and I had had a disagreement, and he'd received what he felt was an unjust punishment. He looked at me sternly and said, "Mommy, I am very mad with you."

I looked at him sympathetically. "Oh, Mike, I'm sorry. I guess we won't be cuddling tonight."

He frowned and quickly amended his indictment: "Well, I'm *sad* with you, then." He wasn't about to jeopardize the most important part of his day!

In the heat of the battle, parents often forget the most critical component of effective parenting: if you don't have the kind of relationship with your child that he or she wants to preserve, you have no leverage. As a child, what do I have to gain by obeying you if you're always yelling at me anyway? What's the upside? On the other hand, if I really enjoy spending time with you when I'm not in trouble, I'll do my best to stay on your good side. The bonus here is that you don't have to be the best parent in the neighborhood; you don't have to be the most creative, energetic, or intelligent adult in your child's life. If you work at keeping a healthy relationship, your child will have the best reason in the world to obey you and follow your guidance.

In a nutshell, here's what your strong-willed children need in their relationship with you:

- *Rules are only what I do. What matters is not what but who.* Relationships will always matter more to me than rules. If I have a good relationship with you, I'll follow your rules even when I don't agree with them. I do it because I love and respect you.
- *No matter where or how far I roam, I always know what to count on at home.* Home should be a place I'll always look forward to coming back to, a safe harbor where I am understood and valued for who I am. I know you want to prepare me for dealing with a hostile world, but if you don't provide a safe warm place for me, who will?
- *Be there for me, no matter what, with "I love you, period," not "I love you, but."* That doesn't mean you should let me take advantage of you. It means your love for me is unshakeable and unconditional. That same love must sometimes be tough, and it doesn't just bail me out when I get in trouble. But above all, no matter what I say or do, I have to know your love for me will never disappear.

Critical Element 2: Awareness and Understanding

Relationship is the first critical element, but there's an equally important second one: an awareness and understanding of how the strong-willed mind works.

Of course, you say, I already know how a strong-willed mind works; I live in one! Then this next section should come as no surprise to you. Let me remind you of five major reasons strong-willed kids get in trouble.

Lack of Interest

Boredom is our greatest enemy. The mind of a strong-willed individual is in perpetual motion, constantly scanning the horizon for new challenges, interesting tasks, and exciting conquests. Now, put that mind in a standard classroom with a textbook and a teacher who is lecturing in a monotone voice, and you've got trouble! A question frequently asked by strong-willed kids, especially when it comes to school, is, "What's the point?" Why do twenty-five math problems if you've mastered the concept after doing the first five? Why read the assigned textbook if the teacher's just going to lecture on the same thing anyway? We don't do well with explanations like "Do it because I said so" or "Just do it so you can get an A." We have little patience for anything that seems like a waste of time.

Sounds familiar, doesn't it? You remember your childhood? But now you're in the opposite position. You've become the parent who must somehow justify the hoops that need to be jumped through in order to survive boring experiences like school. How will you convince your indifferent protégé that much of life must be tackled whether it's interesting or not? Think about it. What would work for you? Most strong-willed folks will tell you that honesty goes a long way. Don't try so hard to talk us into enjoying a task if you know it's only a hoop. Be up front with us; commiserate and sympathize; let us know it's okay not to love it, then calmly hold us accountable.

Lack of Motivation

I've always loved the Charles Schultz cartoon where Charlie Brown has his head in his hands and says, "There's no heavier burden than a great potential!" Can't you just hear your parents telling you, "You are capable of so much better than this!" or "You know you could have straight A's if you put your mind to it!" We could always do better if we wanted to, but therein lies the secret—getting us to want to.

I read a newspaper article proudly announcing that every human brain was created with the potential to master advanced calculus. It was obvious these researchers were wildly enthusiastic about their findings, sure that this discovery would infuse new confidence in every student who struggles with math. Excuse me, but just because my mind is *capable* of doing advanced calculus doesn't mean I have the slightest interest in exploring that possibility. The trouble is, the brighter and more intelligent you are, the more your parents and teachers try to get you to do what *they* think is best, and half the time they don't even ask if that's what you want.

The key to motivating a strong-willed child is to get that strong-willed child to motivate himself. Instead of saying, "This grade has to come up!" ask "Is this the grade you wanted?" After all, you can't make me want a better grade. On the other hand, if *I* say I want to do better, we both have something to work with. If I say I don't want a better grade (and that's usually just to test you), you may have to just drop the whole issue and come back to it later. Ask more questions: Do you want to get a higher-paying job? Is this what you want your room to look like? What kind of grades do you think you'll need to go to college? I know it will be hard, but sometimes you have to back up a little and make sure everyone has a mutual goal before you put the ball in play.

Perceived Lack of Trust

Jackie was a senior in high school, and she needed five dollars to put gas in her car. Her mom was on her way out for the evening and had only a ten-dollar bill. No problem, Jackie told her, she'd just take the ten and bring five back. Her mom hesitated. She didn't really want to do that, she said. Jackie couldn't believe it. Didn't her mom trust her? Before her mom could even answer the charge, Jackie was storming down the hall to her room. "How can you even trust me to be in your house?" she screamed. Her mother stood speechless as Jackie hurled the last threat. "Well, I just won't be here when you get home!" She slammed her bedroom door and began to pack. By the time her mother got back that evening, Jackie was gone—bag and baggage. Jackie is a grown woman with her own daughter now, but she remembers that confrontation like it was yesterday. She readily admits it was crazy to move out over five dollars, but she can still recall the outrage she felt at the perception of being trusted so little that her mother wouldn't lend her a ten-dollar bill.

Obviously, not every situation will get as out of control as Jackie's, but every strong-willed child can understand the frustration felt when those who are supposed to love you most won't automatically believe the best in you. Whenever possible, especially in minor issues, make it a point to show your strong-willed

---

In Her Own Words

Without a doubt it is that I tend to try to think for everyone else as well! I try to control others' behaviors and thoughts. And in the past I have reacted poorly when they did not respond the way I would've liked them to. So the most trouble is in close relationships where I am too controlling.

— ANONYMOUS

---

child you're willing to give her the benefit of the doubt. Unless she proves she can't live up to your trust, find as many ways as you can to emphasize how much you appreciate her reliability.

Lack of Control

Susan was less than four weeks away from high school graduation. In addition to perfecting her basketball skills, her grades had been very good, and she not only had been accepted to the college of her choice but also had received at least three different scholarships. The future looked bright right up until fifth period English on Thursday afternoon. Lunch was over and Susan was sitting in her desk holding her ever-present basketball, waiting for the teacher to arrive. As the minutes ticked by, Susan absentmindedly dribbled her basketball on the floor beside her desk. Suddenly, her teacher's face loomed above her, and he looked angry. He grabbed her basketball and pointed his finger in Susan's face. "Young lady, you will write me a thousand-word essay on why it is inappropriate to dribble a basketball in English class, and you will turn it in to me by Monday morning."

Well, to make a long story short, Susan refused to write the essay. She argued that it was a huge waste of time and a dumb assignment, and she just wasn't going to do it. Her teacher was furious and told Susan and her parents that unless her essay was turned in by Monday, she would receive a failing grade in English for the semester, which meant she would not graduate. Susan said that was just fine with her, and her mother frantically appealed to the principal for help. Fortunately, this wise man was able to negotiate a last-minute compromise. Susan agreed to write an essay, but it would be on the topic of her choice. The teacher agreed to accept the essay as long as it was the required length, was well written, and was turned in on time.

Every strong-willed child quickly figures out that no one else has ultimate control over what you do if you're willing to die for it. Cut off my nose to spite my face? Daily minor surgery! Any time you come at me with a bony finger in my face saying phrases like "you must," "you will," and "you have to," be prepared to watch me fight to the death to prove I still have control of the situation. It doesn't mean I have to control you. I just can't let you take all control away from me. If you can find a way for me to share the control, I'll usually do what you wanted me to in the first place.

Perceived Lack of Authority

She was a beautiful little girl, probably around four or five years old, and she was sitting in her mother's shopping cart in Target, lovingly holding a package containing a brand new Barbie doll. Mom was looking in office supplies, where I stood and overheard this great example of strong-willed parenting.

The girl began loudly complaining. "I'm bored, Mommy— I'm really bored. Let's go—I'm bored! I said I want to go *now!*"

Her mother looked at her calmly and said, "If you keep complaining, we'll just leave right now and go straight home."

Her daughter looked at her slyly as she smugly said, "We won't leave without paying for this stuff."

Her mother didn't miss a beat. Without raising her voice, she replied quietly, "But we *will* be leaving without Barbie."

Her daughter immediately fell silent. Chalk one up for Mom!

Strong-willed children don't usually struggle with authority, only with how that authority is communicated. If you are

In Her Own Words

I have survived so many difficult times, and continue to do so, that I wonder if a lesser-willed person could have endured them. I have had family members and friends tell me they don't know how I could survive being a single mom with three boys, let alone all four of us strong-willed in a tiny four-room house. They have said, "I don't know how you do it," as if they couldn't if they were in my position. I don't know that that is true, because you don't know what you can handle until you are handed it. Now I thank God for my strong will, strong heart, and strong body. He knew I couldn't give up on my life. He tests my strength every day, it seems, especially with my boys. There have been times when I haven't wanted a strong will. I want to walk away and quit. But I can't. God gave me a task I can't refuse.

— MKMKSMITH

strong, reasonable, and calm, and you do what you say you'll do, you'll find that your strong-willed son or daughter will respect your authority. If you seem weak, tentative, or uncertain when you deal with them, they'll move in for the kill, so to speak. It isn't your anger but your action that makes all the difference.

For a whole book of ideas and strategies that will help you bring out the best in your strong-willed child, read *You Can't Make Me! (But I Can Be Persuaded)*. In the meantime, here are a few quick points to remember when it comes to dealing with those kids who think so much like you do!

Strong-Willed Infants and Toddlers

I seek to control whatever part of myself or my environment that I can.

I learned at eighteen months that they can't make you digest peas. They can pry your little mouth open and put the peas in, and you may accidentally swallow a couple, but it is you and you alone who decides whether they stay down or they come back up. This is an amazing discovery for a strong-willed toddler! My parents may be ten times stronger or older or smarter, but there are certain things they just can't make me do!

It doesn't take me long to find out that I can exercise control over what I do and do not *have* to do. Potty training? No matter how important it is to my mom, I still have the last word. Time out? Well, you may have to stand on the other side of the door the whole time to keep me in that room. Wear the clothes you put on me? You can't hold me every second, and I can take those clothes off in the blink of an eye. It seems like a game at first, but I learn very early that my parents often don't have much of a sense of humor! I was just testing to see what I could and couldn't do, but now my mom's yelling at me and pointing her finger in my face and demanding I do it or else. Or else what? What's she going to do? She just said I was going to do something and *she means it!* But she's not the boss of me! I can just sit here and refuse to move. I can kick and scream when she picks me up and tries to make me move. Then the minute she lets loose of me, I can go back to being where I was before. It's no longer fun, but now she made me mad, and I can't let her push me around like this!

Sound familiar? From the very beginning, your strong-willed offspring will be figuring out what the boundaries are and how much of their universe they can control. If you're a strong-willed mom, you know better than anyone why this is happening, but it's sure not the same when you're the parent instead of the child!

Figure out as early as possible how you can voluntarily give your child some control over himself, even in very small ways. Don't just give her the toy you want her to have; let her have a choice. If he's determined to walk up those stairs without you, hang close enough to ensure his safety, but let him take the time he needs to struggle up a step at a time. If she wants to carry that dirty ragged blanket into church, swallow your pride and let it go. There will be some very important battles you will need to fight over physical safety and moral or spiritual values. To maintain your parental authority, you need to learn when to share that all-important control. Choose your battles early, and the seas of childhood will stay much calmer!

The Elementary Years

I'm trying to figure out why I have to do something just because you said so.

Why do I have to keep my room clean? Why do I have to do that stupid homework? Why do I even have to go to school when I don't learn anything anyway? By the time I'm in the fourth grade, I've decided I dread going to school every day. Stuff I liked as a kid is so boring to me now, and the reasons my parents give me for doing things are so lame. Why is everyone always telling me to sit still and stop talking? Why can't you ask any questions? Why do adults get to have the last word anyway? As long as you can reach the pedals, what's so magic about being sixteen before you get to drive a car? Why doesn't anyone want to really sit down and answer my questions?

Whoa—you thought it might get easier as they got older! Childhood is an adventure for your strong-willed child, and you can often find yourself running to keep up. I know—you're the parent and you know best, but that independent, stubborn son or daughter doesn't want to just take your word for it. Unfortunately these are usually the busiest years, with working parents and soccer games and baseball practice and choir performances and teacher conferences. It would make life so much easier if your children would just do what you say without the endless arguments and questions! But you know that's not how the strong-willed mind works. If we want to know something, we'll keep up a dogged pursuit of answers until we practically drive you crazy. How will you cope?

Here's where it is especially important to remember a question I mentioned earlier in the chapter: What's the point? Instead of dealing with endless and pointlessly detailed questions, just cut to the chase; give them the bottom line. "Look, here's the deal. The bottom line is that your homework has to be done by 8 A.M. tomorrow morning. If you want to wake up an hour early to do it, that's fine. If you want to do it in ten-minute sessions, that's fine, too. But at eight in the morning, the homework has to be done." "You don't want to do the dishes? Fine. But everyone has a chore to do. Maybe you can get your sister to trade with you tonight." Don't engage in arguments over methods; focus on the outcomes. Try writing the question on a piece of paper and taping it to your refrigerator: What's the point? It won't stop all the questions, but it sure will go a long way toward giving shorter answers.

The Teenage Years

Leave me alone—but don't go away!

"You're not wearing *that*, are you?" "You better watch your mouth." "You'll never get to college with these grades!" How often did you hear those statements when you were a teenager? There's something about adolescence that makes us believe everyone is constantly bugging us about everything. We're trying to establish our independence and individuality, but it seems like all the authority figures in our lives are just trying to keep their thumb on us. When are they going to trust us? When will they finally leave us alone? It's not that we want to completely be free of our family; after all, there are lots of perks to living at home. We enjoy the laundry service, the good meals, and the financial underwriting of many projects. But why can't we have things our way sometimes? When are you going to treat us like grown-ups? Not every strong-willed teenager is destined to become rebellious or difficult to live with, but when a wild streak sets in, even the strongest-willed mom can face some daunting challenges.

As you know, there aren't many simple answers, but there are a couple of tried-and-true guidelines that can really help keep peace and harmony in the family:

Guide—Don't Dictate

Every teenager needs to know how to motivate himself before he leaves home. Instead of telling your teenager what to do and how to do it, decide together what needs to be accomplished, and ask your son or daughter what it will take to motivate him or her to do it. She needs to be thinking about what it will take to get herself to do something she doesn't want to do. Don't just automatically step in and give advice and suggestions like you did when he was younger. Ask him what he wants to do and what he thinks it will take to get the job done. You're needed more now as a guide and resource than a supervisor and taskmaster. There will still be issues you'll go to the wall for, but choosing your battles is more important now than ever.

Share the Problem

We do better with compelling problems to solve than with a list of chores to do. Instead of just handing down the to-do lists and issuing the rules and regulations, try soliciting input from a very creative and often untapped source—your strong-willed teenager. Put forth the compelling problem you need to have solved, and be sincere and open-minded when you ask for input. You already know what you want to have done, but what if there's another way to accomplish the same goal? Share the problem, and you may be surprised at how quickly and willingly your teen will help you get the job done.

The Strong-Willed Adult Child

Is it my imagination, or are more kids staying at home well into adulthood? I left home for college, but I kept coming back. It was a great compliment to my parents, actually, since home has always been a place I look forward to visiting. It was a welcome harbor when I felt battered by the storms of life, and it always promised a warm meal and a functioning laundry room. When I was single, I'd move into a new apartment for a year, accumulate a little too much debt, then move into my parents'

Put This on Your Refrigerator!

Regardless of my age, you can almost always count on trouble if you ...

> try to take all control away from me.
>
> issue orders and ultimatums like you're the big boss.
>
> attempt to negotiate from a position of weakness.
>
> don't follow through with promised consequences (a deal's a deal).
>
> only try to motivate me to do what you want me to do.
>
> yell at me instead of calmly carrying out your discipline.
>
> forget to smile at me and remind me you still love me.

---

basement for a few months to catch up on my bills and strike out on my own again. Although I've always gotten along well with my parents, we all had adjustments to make when I moved back home as an adult. You can't exactly give a twenty-four-year-old a curfew, but it's unrealistic to think your parents won't worry when you haven't shown up or called after midnight. As long as you are in their home, they still have a right to expect certain courtesies and behaviors. That's where it gets pretty tricky.

Especially for a strong-willed parent, it's very tempting to keep exercising control over your children, even after they're adults. You may look forward to spending time with them as friends, rather than in the former parent-child relationship, but you can also find yourselves in uncomfortable situations if you aren't careful about respecting each other's independence and individual space. In the end, you're the one who will need to surrender control and be willing to let your adult children succeed or fail on their own merits. That may sound easy, but to those of us who have cherished having control for eighteen years, it may take several years of practice!

part 3

The Strong-Willed Woman at Work

chapter 7

Strong-Willed Women in the Workplace

So here's what I want you to do, God helping you: Take your everyday, ordinary life—your sleeping, eating, going-to-work, and walking-around life—and place it before God as an offering.

—Romans 12:1

I had a real eye-opening experience during the year I did my student teaching at a local public high school. I expected to be spending time with teachers who were enthusiastically dedicated to a lifelong passion for instructing young minds. But it turned out there weren't very many of those. There were far more school district employees who came to work and simply did the job they were paid to do. They weren't incompetent or unpleasant; they just seemed complacent and resigned. I couldn't help but express my surprise, and one of the veteran teachers decided to fill me in. "Listen, kid," he said, "you'll learn soon enough that you'll just burn yourself out trying to stay excited about your job all the time. Pace yourself, and just go with the flow. You get summers off, you have a retirement plan and a benefits package—what more do you want?" Even though I don't believe he is necessarily typical of most teachers, he sure helped my resolve never to have just "a job." Maybe it was my youth, but I cared passionately about my work, and I couldn't imagine staying in a job I didn't just love.

Are you in the right job? I believe the majority of strong-willed women would say they are now, or that they're on their way to getting the right job. I've never spoken to a strong-willed woman who complained of living a life of "quiet desperation." As a rule, we don't have the patience or mindset to stay in a job we hate unless it's part of a strategy for getting where we want to be. That doesn't mean we stay in one ideal job forever; most strong-willed women tend to have multiple jobs in their life-times. Many of us hold down two or three jobs simultaneously, especially when we're younger. It also doesn't mean that every job we have is to our liking; some may be distasteful jobs, but they're temporary. We can do anything we set our minds to do when we need to do it—for a while. Maybe you're not in that ideal job yet. You might even be right in the middle of one of those frustrating jobs that seems to be sapping your energy and enthusiasm. Take heart—you're certainly not alone out there! But you do have a distinct advantage over other women who don't share your same degree of strong will. You do not have to stay trapped in an undesirable job forever, and your job is not your entire life.

Perspective Points

You can keep your perspective and your momentum if you keep at least two points in mind.

Long-Term Goals

Always keep your long-term goal in view, but be prepared for God to have another idea. I still remember, as I started my freshman year of college, standing in the middle of the campus and reminding God of my lifelong dream: I wanted to be a writer. Perhaps I could be an editor of a prominent national magazine on my way to becoming a successful novelist or journalist. It certainly sounded a lot more glamorous than becoming a teacher, which seemed to be where God was nudging me. I must confess I was a little disappointed when it became clear to me that I needed to be a high school English teacher instead of just trying to jump into the New York publishing scene.

I was determined to be the best at whatever I did and to stay as diverse as possible, so I threw myself passionately into my teaching, but I learned to do dozens of other part-time and temporary jobs as I fleshed out my resume and work experience. I found out I truly loved teaching, but I wanted to do more to help students succeed. In the midst of two or three side-jobs, I finished my master's degree in learning styles and began to teach seminars and consult with schools and businesses, giving them tools to help even the most reluctant learner succeed. I enjoyed eight years of classroom experience and six years of law enforcement and hundreds of hours of a variety of other occupations, in education, government offices, and corporate America. I got married, lived through John's life-threatening illness less than two years into our marriage, and then became the mother of absolutely incredible red-headed twin boys. Suddenly I had my own in-home laboratory for discovering the uniqueness of each child, even when he's born within two minutes of his brother and is growing up in identical circumstances. I was challenged to apply my learning styles knowledge and experience to parenting, and before I knew it my seminars were expanding.

The twins were only three years old when, out of the blue, I got a phone call from the managing editor at Focus on the Family, one of the most popular and well-loved Christian organizations in broadcasting and publishing. Someone she knew had attended one of my seminars and had shown her some of my handout materials. Would I be interested in putting together a proposal to write a book for Focus on the Family? Well, to make a long story short, my first book, *The Way They Learn,* was released in October 1994, almost twenty years to the day from the time I stood on that college campus and told God I wanted to be a writer. I still smile when I think of it, because I know God must have been saying to me, "What would you have *written* about?" If he had revealed to me that it would take twenty years to reach my goal and make my dream come true, I would have been too discouraged to go on. But he lovingly and skillfully helped to weave a complex and beautiful tapestry, making sure I had all the necessary components to be successful in ways I could never have anticipated.

My story may remind you of an old goal as yet unmet, and you might be ready to resign yourself to the idea that you'll never achieve what you thought you would. But don't be so sure! God has a wonderful way of weaving life experiences into exactly what you need to prepare you for meeting your goals, even if it takes years to see them fulfilled.

Some of you reading this will be that very analytic type of person who actually uses the day planners and keeps a list of daily, monthly, and yearly goals. Some of you will be more like me, just keeping a general sense of where you want to go and knowing that you'll recognize the goal when you see it. Either way, you need to stay confident that you have somewhere to go, a horizon to explore, a challenge to meet. The strong-willed woman is not an aimless wanderer; even working behind the grill at a fast food restaurant is bearable when it's part of the greater plan.

Short-Term Goals

Dealing with the short-term: Never lose sight of the light at the end of the tunnel.

I was finishing my master's degree, teaching high school during the day, and working the streets as a cop at night and on weekends. I was grading papers at stoplights and sleeping less than four hours a night. I had decided I wanted to start my own business as an educational consultant, and true to my nature, I wanted to take the fast track. But I needed to have a job for a while that didn't include as many extra hours as teaching required.

I found a job as a paralegal for a downtown attorney and began the two-year journey toward obtaining my master's degree. The attorney I worked for was wonderful, but the law office as a whole was not a good fit. They were sticklers for clocking in and clocking out, and someone was always looking over my shoulder. I worked quickly and efficiently, but every day someone pulled rank on me.

"Get the client some coffee."

"These copies are too light. Go do them again."

"I told you to make two copies. Go do another one."

I was low on the food chain, so to speak, and I got bossed around every day. I was determined to keep this job; it was the salary I needed and the hours I needed, and I wasn't a quitter. *Two years—just two years,* I told myself, *and then I'll be out of here forever.*

In my learning-styles research, I had discovered evidence that if people have a prolonged and extreme mismatch of learning style, their minds will cause a catastrophe to happen to bring them back in balance—strokes, ulcers, heart attacks, emotional breakdowns. In my case, it was migraine headaches and other physical symptoms. It took every ounce of strength and discipline I had to be a model employee. I got bonuses and awards, and everyone thought I was doing such a great job, but I was going home every day with a stomachache. I used every sick leave day that was coming to me, mostly because of severe migraine headaches and frequent colds and flu.

But I knew the work situation was only temporary. I had already set the date for my resignation, and I could see that light at the end of the tunnel getting closer every week. I made it, and at the end of two years I resigned on good terms and started my own business. Despite the fact I made very little money that first year of self-employment, I didn't have so much as a head cold, let alone a migraine headache.

Your strong will can get you through very tough times at work, but the best chance you have for success is to make sure you keep your eyes on that light at the end of each tunnel.

Our Greatest Work-Place Challenges

When we strong-willed women are at our best, any organization would be lucky to have us. We can work tirelessly to accomplish a task, spread enthusiasm among even the most resistant coworkers, and troubleshoot solutions to problems no

In Her Own Words

Growing up, my mouth could be my own worst enemy. But I've had to learn through many experiences that I needed to be more diplomatic.

My first victory was learning not to respond immediately. Now my best friend teases me because she knows when I'm irritated by things because—according to her—I "blink." What I'm doing is editing: "can't say that, that would be mean, that wouldn't be Christian." It can take a while for me to reply. Now that I've had a little practice, I'm finding that it is easier to remain silent than to apologize. Now all I have to do is get this blinking thing under control.

— LEANNE

one else could solve. There are, however, situations that have the potential to bring out the worst in us, and it's worth taking a look at some of those scenarios that can sabotage our efforts to reflect the best side of our God-given strengths.

Working for a Dictatorial Boss

If you end up working for someone who likes to be "the boss," it may take all the discipline you can muster not to react negatively to "bossiness." Every day can become a tense stand-off when someone who outranks you insists on ordering you around. Remember, as strong-willed women, even simple directives can sound like ultimatums, and we don't react well to bony fingers pointed in our faces. The bottom line is this: if you need to stay in this job, you'll need to find a way to get along with the boss. Be proactive. Start figuring out how you're going to live with this before someone else starts getting you in trouble. I ran across a refrigerator magnet recently that said, "Those who anger you control you." Ouch—that ought to help keep things in perspective!

Working on a Rigid, Inflexible Schedule

There's a big drawback to having a strong-willed, independent spirit; you need to be independent. Unfortunately, unless you're the owner or the boss, someone else usually calls the shots when it comes to setting your schedule. I mentioned earlier that I worked for a wonderful attorney, and one of the things I liked most about him was that he let me persuade him to adjust my schedule. My argument was simple: if the point was getting the work done and I could consistently get it done before 3 P.M., why couldn't I start at 6 A.M., open the office, and start the coffee for everyone else's arrival? I was fortunate to have an open-minded boss. If your arguments for flexible scheduling fall on deaf ears, decide whether keeping the job is worth it. If it is, make up your mind to jump through the necessary hoops

---

In Her Own Words

I won't lie that it sometimes kills me to sit still when I see so much I could do (or so much I could control, lead, and effect). But the Lord is teaching me that the world revolves around him and not me. And that he'll raise up the right leaders (and he does!). And that's been good for me to learn.

—ANONYMOUS

---

until you reach your goal. No one says you have to give up on coming up with creative solutions while you wait, though!

Working with Those Who Don't Share Your Vision or Enthusiasm

Even the most mundane job has possibilities to a creative mind. As you work in that rather boring and routine position on your way to getting the perfect job, you just can't help but look around and wonder how you could improve the circumstances. Your mind is full of ideas, and you know yourself well enough to understand that unless you find a way to make each day more interesting, you're going to get in trouble. But there's one major drawback to your plan: no one else at work seems to care at all about making things better. You could find yourself becoming very impatient and frustrated with your supervisor and coworkers, and before you know it, you have the reputation of being harsh and critical. You just wanted to make their lives *easier!* You wanted to make a difference in a dull drab world. So here's the reality pill again. This job is a stepping stone, a hoop to jump through, and you want to make the best of it while you have to be there. Awareness is half the battle. Knowing why you're frustrated will go a long way toward making the daily grind bearable.

Working with Those Who Move Slowly or Seem to Lack Ambition

When I was in college, one of my summer jobs was for a government agency (which will go unnamed) in Las Vegas, where we lived. I couldn't believe my good fortune at landing a job that would allow me to be part of America's payroll, and I was eager to begin contributing my youthful energy and creativity.

In Her Own Words

Christianity holds me accountable for how I use my strong will. In my youth, like Bam-Bam on "The Flintstones," I did not always understand my own strength, so to speak. I didn't pray for God's guidance when making decisions. I didn't pray to be made aware of offensive ways within me. I didn't realize what amazing strength there is in self-control.

—DCEALLAIGH

My office partner had been working for the agency for several years, and it didn't take long to figure out he thought I was a whirlwind. "Slow down!" he told me. "Relax! What's your hurry? They're paying you for being here. Why do you have to work so hard that you make the rest of us look lazy?"

I was incredulous. Surely people didn't just sit for hours at a time with nothing to do?

He shrugged. "Sometimes," he admitted. "But other times we get the work done. We just don't get too wound up about it."

I was young enough to make waves without realizing there might be repercussions from my colleagues. By the end of the summer, I had completely reorganized the professional library and streamlined the filing for the entire office. My supervisor was delighted, and I received a very nice letter of recommendation. But no one threw me a farewell party, and I was never encouraged to return during my next college break!

Sometimes you will be in the very unpopular position of having to choose between doing your best and fitting in with the rest. I don't have to guess what most of you will end up doing! There will, however, always be a price to pay. I believe it's worth it, but I also know you may have to occasionally tread lightly and speak softly in order to maintain your good standing with your employer. There are times when strong will puts on velvet gloves, but it still keeps a firm grip on integrity.

Do You Know What Your Ideal Job Will Be?

My friend Sam (not his real name) has been a middle school teacher more than twenty years. He's a great teacher and works well with the kids and staff alike. He just finished his degree in counseling and spent a significant amount of time and money to get it. I've worked with Sam and watched as he's achieved various honors and awards. But Sam confided to me he's not really

---

In Her Own Words

My strong will gave me courage to try things exciting, dangerous, and unusual. If something sounded challenging, I would do it. From flying to California to train with the best aerobics leaders in the '80s to working as a set up–take down person for a hot air balloon company. In my midtwenties, I tried out to be a dancer for a semi-pro basketball team. I danced in front of three thousand people. I would try just about anything. But I also got into trouble. I tried all the wrong things, hung out at all the wrong places with all the wrong people. No one could tell me what I was doing was wrong.

—MKMKSMITH

---

in the job he loves the most. One morning at church I was talking to him when he revealed his true dream job.

"You know what I'd really love to do?" he asked me. "I'd love to own an auto junkyard."

I couldn't hide my surprise. I'd never even had the desire to visit an auto junkyard.

He had a dreamy look in his eyes as he continued. "Yeah, my dad and I almost bought one when I was younger, and I've thought about it ever since. The only trouble is, I wouldn't want to *sell* anything. I'd just spend my days walking around among the cars, and I wouldn't want to let anything go."

And that's when it really hit me. God puts in every heart a deep desire and calling, and every one of us is uniquely qualified to answer our call. What seems undesirable to one is just the right fit for the other. We use a septic tank company owned by a man who just loves his work. I met a woman who absolutely lives for packaging pieces of candy on an assembly line. Where would we be if someone didn't have a vision for trash collection? As a man *or* woman in the workplace, the most important job we have is finding what we are truly supposed to be doing with our lives. It isn't always a grandiose position or even a management-level career. It may or may not involve national acclaim or world-changing ideas. But this one thing I know: God has a plan for me, and—with every fiber of my strong-willed being—I want to find and follow his will.

chapter 8

Strong-Willed Women in Leadership

Make a careful exploration of who you are and the work you have been given, and then sink yourself into that. Don't be impressed with yourself. Don't compare yourself with others. Each of you must take responsibility for doing the creative best you can with your own life.
                                        —Galatians 6:3–4

One afternoon a big wolf waited in a dark forest for a little girl to come along carrying a basket of food to her grandmother. Finally, a little girl did come along and she was carrying a basket of food. 'Are you carrying that basket to your grandmother?' asked the wolf. The little girl said yes, she was. So the wolf asked her where her grandmother lived and the little girl told him and he disappeared into the wood.

"When the little girl opened the door of her grandmother's house she saw that there was somebody in bed with a nightcap and nightgown on. She had approached no nearer than twenty-five feet from the bed when she saw that it was not her grandmother but the wolf, for even in a nightcap a wolf does not look any more like your grandmother than the Metro-Goldwyn lion looks like Calvin Coolidge. So the little girl took an automatic out of her basket and shot the wolf dead.

"Moral: *It is not so easy to fool little girls nowadays as it used to be.*"[1]

No one would dispute that the role of women in our society is constantly evolving and changing. When we think about women in leadership roles, we tend to focus on the differences between a man and a woman. True leadership ability, however, is not confined to either gender. The equal rights and feminist movement has often put a distinctly negative spin on women's issues in the workplace. It seems the media is constantly digging up studies and examples of "glass ceilings," working moms who get fewer benefits, and the gap in pay between the sexes. While these issues are important, I fear they have been used to distract us from the timeless and universal characteristics of a genuine leader—regardless of gender.

What Message Are We Sending?

I wonder if some of us strong-willed women, looking for any sign that someone might be treating us unfairly, have been quick to highlight deficiencies and slow to affirm progress. In many ways, we've made the male population more than a little paranoid when it comes to dealing with a woman who wants to scale the ladder of corporate success.

Over many years, I have been to dozens of workshops and seminars about "cultural diversity" and "gender sensitivity." For the most part, my colleagues and I, especially in law enforcement and the public service fields, left feeling more paranoid than ever. It certainly didn't make us want to seek out and appreciate the

In Her Own Words

I can lead effectively. And I can follow effectively. But I have a problem with co-leading. People drive me nuts (which is probably why I work professionally with computers; I can turn them off when they irritate me). However, lots of people enjoy working with me (especially people who want to develop more leadership qualities ... what do they see?). I'm told I'm competent and well-prepared for things and that I take things seriously.

— ANONYMOUS

diversity in people around us. Instead, we were almost hoping we *didn't* run into anyone significantly different. What if we said the wrong thing? What if we didn't remember to say the right thing? There was always the danger of pulling up to the scene of a crime and, instead of focusing on doing our jobs, being preoccupied with limiting our liability. I think it's getting a little ridiculous when we have to worry more about equality than outcomes.

Instead of appreciating our leadership skills as women, men have had to protect themselves from discrimination lawsuits. Rather than enjoying our company, they have had to guard their words and actions against potential sexual harassment charges. I don't want to be made a leader because I am a woman and you need more women to even things out. I want to be a leader because I'm the best man for the job.

I am absolutely in favor of protecting civil rights, and I do not condone discrimination, but I don't see a clear and fair definition being used. Speaking as the "minority" called women, I don't want standards to be lowered or exceptions to be made to accommodate me in the workplace. I don't want to achieve rank or status based upon an unfair advantage over someone inherently more qualified. I want there to be a clear and solid definition of what needs to be done, and if I can do it, I want the chance to prove it. As tempting as it is to use my gender to get special loans and grants for women-owned businesses, it shouldn't be necessary. If I have a solid business plan and a good track record, why do I have to be a woman to get the bank's attention?

I picked up an anthology of business advice compiled by a Christian publishing company. They offered excerpts and essays from sixteen "respected leaders" offering biblical wisdom and business insights. Out of the sixteen, only two were women. Most of the Fortune 500 business seminars feature outstanding leaders and CEOs as speakers, and I've never seen more than one or two women in the lineup. Should we assume women are being left out because of their gender, or are there simply more men in that particular population? The bottom line is, we strong-willed women should fight to make sure women have the same opportunities as their male counterparts, but if we cannot prove that we can meet or exceed expectations and outcomes, the best person for the job should win. Period.

Gender Matters

Communicating a Message

I believe God calls us, whether men or women, to where he most needs us. There are both men and women who have the ability to reach the entire population with their message, but we shouldn't assume that everyone is equally capable of understanding and appreciating us just because we want to be heard. The apostle Paul says this: "If *I* don't understand the language, it's not going to do me much good. It's no different with you. Since you're so eager to participate in what God is doing, why don't you concentrate on doing what helps everyone in the church?" (1 Corinthians 14:11–12). Some outstanding women leaders, both in business and in ministry, are not gifted in effectively reaching both men and women with their message. It doesn't mean they shouldn't be in leadership, but it does mean they need to be sensitive to where God can best use their talents. There's no doubt that men and women each need their own voice. It's why Promise Keepers is so effective in men's ministry and Women of Faith and Renewing the Heart provide wonderful venues for women across the nation.

There may be times when we just have to know and appreciate where we can do the most good. We don't have to please everybody, but we can't afford not to please God!

In Her Own Words

I find that a lot of men in leadership positions in church are threatened by me. They are usually married to fairly meek women, and I must either come as a complete surprise or a total nightmare! I have found that the more "submissive" the woman (outwardly, that is . . .), the more respected she is in the church and especially by the leadership. It doesn't matter how creative I am or how innovative my ideas, if it rocks the boat or threatens a position held by a man, then I'd best forget it.

—ANONYMOUS

Understanding Need

There are times when men can be more effective than women, and vice versa. Like it or not, there are certain situations in which it really makes a difference whether a man or a woman is performing a job. There are the obvious examples like airport security screening, body searches in prison, and PE teachers supervising in the locker rooms. But there are also the less obvious times when people just need to communicate with someone like themselves.

I clearly remember an incident when I was still very new to the police department. I was so proud of my uniform, my badge, and my status as a fully commissioned police officer. I was working a shift alone one evening when I got a call to go and take a stolen property report. When I arrived, a man in his mid to late sixties was nervously pacing in his front yard. He immediately came out to greet me, obviously relieved the police had come so quickly. But as soon as he got a closer look at me, his whole demeanor changed. "You're not a policeman," he growled. "You're a woman. I want a *real* policeman."

I was stunned, then I was angry. How dare he talk to me that way? Didn't he realize I was going to do a bang-up job of taking that report and starting the investigation to find his treasured possession? But I bit my tongue. This man was very distraught, and he had no intention of letting me help him. I could make a big deal of it, but how would it make the department look? What kind of public image would I be serving?

I struggled to use my kindest voice and told him I would call another officer, but it would mean a longer wait.

"That's fine with me," he said, "just get me a *man* who knows what he's doing." Stung by his words, I radioed for another officer and went back to my patrol car.

It was a humbling experience, but I believe God was showing me that I was part of a much bigger picture. The job I was doing wasn't about me. I was part of something much bigger than that. I could have made a big deal about the fact that I was equally qualified; I could have pointed out how his prejudice and bias against women was out of line. But the one thing I seek to do more than anything is to bring honor and glory to God. By stepping back in this instance, I chose to avoid the confrontation that could have had a significant negative impact on the police department I worked for and, more important, on the reflection of Christ in my life.

What If I Want to Be in Charge?

Not all strong-willed women need to be in charge all the time. We certainly want to stay involved and have our input valued, but we don't have to run *everything*. That said, I have to admit that most of us would at least like to be *asked* to run everything! We don't want to be considered pushy or obnoxious, so what's the best way to let the world know that we are eminently qualified and eager to step up and lead? There are at least three considerations: attitude, accountability, and action.

Attitude

I can still remember the day my dad came home and gathered the family around him to make an announcement. I was only in elementary school, but I'll never forget his message. He had been reading Norman Vincent Peale's *The Power of Positive Thinking* and had just returned from a workshop. "From now on," he proclaimed, "we are a positive-thinking family. We will

---

In Her Own Words

I'm definitely not a follower. I have to do things that make
sense to me and are consistent with my values.

— ANONYMOUS

---

not speak in negative terms about ourselves or anyone else, and we will think and believe the best in every situation." While that sounded pretty good, we didn't realize at the time how it was about to change our entire lives. Anytime I started to ask Dad a question that began with "I don't suppose I could . . ." he would interrupt me with, "No. Anytime you start with a negative approach, the answer will always be negative."

We had a piggy bank on the kitchen table where we had to deposit a nickel each time we said something negative about someone else. It didn't take long to realize we were *all* going to be broke! We changed the plan and made a pact that if we were going to say something about another person that wasn't positive, we also had to say three *nice* things about them. I have to admit that at first I found myself not saying something *bad* about a person just because I couldn't think of three *good* things! But my father was determined to change our course, and before long, thinking positively became an ingrained pattern.

I can't begin to tell you what a difference that has made in my life. No matter the odds, regardless of the obstacles, my dad taught me the motto "It's always worth a try."

As I grew older, I also realized that people like having a leader who is a positive thinker. They appreciate the person who sees possibilities instead of roadblocks, and they know they can count on finding an upside to every hardship. Even on my most difficult days, the positive attitude my dad instilled in me keeps me on track when others just pull over and give up.

Accountability

The police sergeant and I were sitting in the living room of a grief-stricken mom and dad. Their daughter had been killed in an accident on her way to the prom with her date, who was driving while drunk, and we were there to deliver her personal effects. Although her mom couldn't bring herself to speak, her dad needed to tell us how proud he was of his seventeen-year-old daughter. She was a real leader, he assured us. She led her youth group at church and had a music ensemble that visited the nursing home. Her grades in school were excellent, and she had big plans for the future. She had a real mind of her own, he admitted, but she always used her talents to lead the way for others. He looked at us, puzzled. He said he just couldn't figure out why she would have connected with this boy who was walking on the wild side. His daughter, he said firmly, would never be caught drinking or ducking out of the prom.

I sat there praying he wouldn't ask us the next question, but he did. His daughter hadn't been drinking, had she? I watched his face as the sergeant regretfully informed him that her blood had been tested and the alcohol level was significantly above the legal limit. The shock and surprise gave way to unbearable grief as he sobbed uncontrollably.

Over the next few days, he and his wife discovered many unpleasant aspects of their daughter's secret life, which she had managed to keep very well hidden. I'm sure she was counting on having a chance to explain. I feel certain she wasn't planning to lead a double life forever. But much too soon the unthinkable happened, and what was left behind could no longer be hidden. Every leader needs someone to whom she will be accountable. Even very small secrets have a way of taking on a life of their own and overcoming even the best intentions. As a strong-willed woman who seeks to honor God in all she does, I must find a way to constantly keep myself accountable, not only to God but to those whom I would lead. One strong-willed woman puts it this way:

> I have also learned the importance of being accountable to those over whom I have authority or power. In my former company I asked those who worked closely with me to feel free to tell me when I was doing something they didn't think was right. I even set up review sessions so that we had a formal time for my review as well as theirs.
>
> I try not to close my door or hide my actions from the people who work for me. I want to remember that my words are being heard by them and that I have asked them to hold me accountable. I have been fortunate to have employees who have taken this request seriously and have, from time to time, suggested that I am acting out of anger or have cut a corner I shouldn't have.
>
> Leslie, who as my vice president in my publishing company, was an especially sensitive and committed friend who very gently pointed out things in my life from time to time. Besides being grateful for her professionally, I will always be indebted to her for the times she helped guide me back to the path I had strayed from.[2]

Action

On Saturday of the week in which I had completed a full day refresher course in first aid and CPR training, my sister and I were waiting to be seated for lunch at a nice restaurant.

Suddenly, there was a loud crash and a bloodcurdling scream in the kitchen. "Help! Call 911—she's not breathing!" someone was shouting.

Everyone in the restaurant froze. My heart began to race. Oh no—I wasn't ready for this! Surely there would be someone in the back who could help. I felt God's elbow nudge me. I asked the hostess, "Do you have someone back there who knows first aid and CPR?"

Her face went blank with fear. "I . . . I think so," she stammered. "I . . . I'm not sure."

I hesitated for a moment, but another scream came from the kitchen. I held up the handy little pouch on my key chain that contained a disposable mask for giving artificial respiration. "Would you like me to see if I can help?" I asked.

"Oh, yes!" she said and ushered me quickly back to the kitchen. I have to tell you I felt anything but confident, but no one else seemed to know what to do. There in the kitchen stood six or seven employees in a semicircle, all wringing their hands and crying while a young lady lay on the floor in the middle of a grand mal seizure. I checked, and she was breathing, so I had someone find a towel to cushion her head and bring others to protect her body from the hot stove she fell against. Just then another restaurant patron rushed in and joined me on the floor, talking to the patient comfortingly. During the five or six minutes it took for the aid unit to arrive, not one restaurant employee stepped forward unless we asked them to. Not one had any idea what to do in this kind of emergency.

I was certainly not a hero; I was just the first person to step up and take action. Anyone can stand around hoping someone will know what to do. Every strong-willed woman I know is at least willing to do *something*. As a result of that day, I am making arrangements to do a few ride-alongs with the fire department aid unit so I can be better trained and feel more confident in the next life or death situation I might encounter.

What Kind of Leader Will a Strong-Willed Woman Be?

I like Max DePree's observation about it in his book *Leadership Is an Art:* "The signs of outstanding leadership appear primarily among the followers. Are the followers reaching their potential? Are they learning? Serving? Do they achieve the required results? Do they change with grace? Manage conflict?"[3] Ouch! Looking at my effectiveness as a leader from that perspective isn't always encouraging!

For Whom Do I Lead?

Whether it's in the secular corporate world or in Christian ministry, my calling to be a leader isn't about me. It's about bringing honor and glory to my Boss, the one who is the only

---

In Her Own Words

I hate meetings, mostly because no one shows up prepared and I find it irritating to sit around when we all have other things to do. I lead without a ton of meetings. As VBS director, I've held only one meeting per year, and the program is successful for our small congregation!

—ANONYMOUS

---

employer who can promise eternal compensation. In the end, the only kind of leader that counts is the one who very deliberately follows in the footsteps of Jesus Christ. Max Lucado is one of my favorite authors, and I love the point he makes in his book *America Looks Up* when he talks about our human need for demanding that justice be done. Instead of putting ourselves in the position of deciding for ourselves who should get what, he reminds us of what Jesus says in Matthew:

> It stops when you take seriously the words of Jesus: "For if you forgive men when they sin against you, your heavenly Father will also forgive you. But if you do not forgive men their sins, your Father will not forgive your sins." (Matthew 6:14–15 NIV) "Treat me as I treat my neighbor." Are you aware that this is what you are saying to your Father? "Give me what I give them. Grant me the same peace I grant others. Let me enjoy the same tolerance I offer." God will treat you the way you treat others. Would you like some peace? Then quit giving your neighbor such a hassle. Want to enjoy God's generosity? Then let others enjoy yours. Would you like assurance that God forgives you? I think you know what you need to do.
>
> That's the kind of leader I want to be—and the only way that can happen is for me to give up my spot in the pilot's seat, move over and let God take control.[4]

part 4

The Strong-Willed
Woman and Her World

chapter 9

Strong-Willed Women and Their Relationship with God

It is clear to us, friends, that God not only loves you very much but also has put his hand on you for something special. When the Message we preached came to you, it wasn't just words. Something happened in you. The Holy Spirit put steel in your convictions.

—1 Thessalonians 1:4–5

It was mere weeks until I graduated from college with my teaching degree, and I was already planning to do what was deemed to be impossible. I had signed on to participate in a month-long mission trip, leaving the day after graduation ceremonies. There were sixteen of us scheduled to travel to the jungles of Belize to build a sanctuary for the Maya and Ketchi Indian tribes. My advisor took me aside and gave me some bad news. If I really wanted to get a teaching job, he said, I couldn't afford to be gone during that first month when almost all the hiring was done. He wanted to support my dedication to missions, but he had to tell me that I could pretty much kiss next year's teaching contract goodbye. I have to admit I hesitated. I knew God had definitely called me to teach; would he make me choose between my career and my missions experience?

You've probably already guessed what happened. I went to Belize, and when I came back I was hired for just the job I wanted within two weeks of my return. It was only the beginning of an adulthood filled with examples of God's faithfulness.

As I mentioned earlier in this book, I came to know Christ early, and I willingly surrendered my strong will to him. Why would someone with such a strong will and deeply ingrained streak of independence be so willing to give it all up? Like most strong-willed women, for me it certainly wasn't the threat of eternal damnation that pushed me down to the altar of salvation. It wasn't lectures from a well-meaning Sunday school teacher or "hellfire and brimstone" preached by a dynamic traveling evangelist. It wasn't even my father's sermons. What drew me to Christ was much more personal. So much of our perception of God and our view of that relationship is determined by the relationship we have had with our parents or guardians. If we have not seen unconditional love demonstrated by those on earth who are supposed to love us most, it's very difficult to imagine how a heavenly Father, whom we have never seen, can offer such a priceless gift.

I was blessed with wonderful parents who, at this writing, have been happily married for fifty years. I grew up listening to my mother and father pray together and watched their lives as they put God first, no matter what. My "up close and personal" experience with godly parents showed me that serving Christ is the most important thing I would ever do. Many of you did not have an ideal upbringing. That certainly makes surrendering to Christ more challenging, but not impossible. Many strong-willed women have grown up under the thumb of a rigid and unforgiving interpretation of the Bible or the stern and unyielding discipline of an overly zealous religious parent. Some of you, like my dad, came to Christ from a life of deep sin. His family background was peppered with divorce, dysfunction, alcoholic parents, and "wine, women, and song." He did not experience unconditional love from his parents; his conversion to Christianity precipitated his being officially disowned by his entire family. Instead of using this as an excuse to turn against God, he used his strong will to follow God's leading into full-time ministry, and his daily prayers for the family that rejected him resulted in his father's salvation six months before he died, forty-one years later. No matter what your background, God can work with your strong will to bring you to him, so stay tuned.

Three Key Words

In chapter 1, I mentioned Emily, who couldn't believe there was anything about Christianity that would appeal to her strong-willed nature. She was sure she would have to completely give up her identity as a strong-willed woman if she accepted Jesus Christ as her Savior. I can't tell you what a joy it was to shatter Emily's image of a God who wanted to change her against her will.

Just in case you've ever felt like Emily, or know someone who does, let me tell you what irresistibly drew this iron-willed woman to completely surrender her life to her Designer. It is not my intention to get into any theological debates, since there are thousands of books you can read that deal specifically with this subject. But speaking strictly in layman's terms, there were three words that Emily discovered had different meanings than she had originally thought: repentance, submission, obedience.

Repentance

To the strong-willed woman, *repentance* is a word charged with a lot of negative meaning. The Bible is very clear in its direction that the only way to God is through Jesus Christ and that for him to enter our hearts we must repent of our sins. Emily struggled with this because she had seen so many people walk to the altar so many times, begging God to forgive them and vowing to sin no more. She said she knew they'd be back— they always were—and they'd cry again and repent again, and what good would it do? Was it really that easy? Could you just sin as much as you wanted and then feel bad enough about it that God would forgive you if you repented? That seems like a pretty weak-willed existence. But that's not what repentance means. Here's how Eugene Peterson describes it in his book *A Long Obedience in the Same Direction:*

In Her Own Words

All of us, not just we strong-willed women, are naturally defiant toward God before his spirit draws us to himself and we are radically changed. We strong-willed women just have a different sin-pattern with which to deal: that of trying to control not only our lives but those of our families, colleagues, and friends. Running to Jesus in repentance is an everyday necessity so that we can love and forgive others in the way Jesus loves and forgives us.

—SHARON HALL

> Repentance is not an emotion. It is not feeling sorry for your
> sins. It is a decision. It is deciding that you have been wrong
> in supposing that you could manage your own life and be
> your own god; it is deciding that you were wrong in think-
> ing that you had, or could get, the strength, education and
> training to make it on your own; it is deciding that you have
> been told a pack of lies about yourself and your neighbors
> and your world. And it is deciding that God in Jesus Christ is
> telling you the truth. Repentance is a realization that what
> God wants from you and what you want from God are not
> going to be achieved by doing the same old things, thinking
> the same old thoughts. Repentance is a decision to follow
> Jesus Christ and become his pilgrim in the path of peace.[1]

Nothing weak about that! Repentance means strong, deci-
sive action, and, as a strong-willed woman, I respect that. It's also
very clear that no one will make you repent. It's strictly your
decision, and the timing is your call. Christ will never knock
down the door of our hearts and insist we let him in. He waits
patiently for us to hand him the key.

Submission

When the Bible talks about wives submitting to their husbands and every follower of Christ submitting to him without
reservation, a strong-willed woman hesitates. Perhaps our society has convinced us that submission is the same as subjugation,
and the thought of just handing over control and meekly following the leader is not appealing in any way. We talked earlier
in the book about the surrender of control to an authority as
our choice, and that's exactly what submission to Christ is all
about. Far from being a defeat, our surrender to Jesus represents
a victory over our selfish wills and desires. Now here's the part

In Her Own Words

Strong-Willed Characteristics without God	Strong-Willed Characteristics with God
Quick to find fault in others	Look at my own faults
Quick to blame others	Search myself
Jealous of others	Happy for the success of others
Defensive	Learn to accept criticism
Wait for others to come	Seek forgiveness first and ask for forgiveness
Worry about my reputation	Worry about character before God
Justify myself	Agree with true condition of my heart
Self-confident	God's power in me
Self-centered	Gratitude overflows in love
Proud	Surrender my will to his
Self-reliant	Cast everything on him
Manifest broken spirits	Manifest mercy
Stir up trouble	Become a peacemaker

—MARY

where you really need your strong will: it will take a lot of discipline on your part to stay submitted on a daily basis. Submission on your part represents the highest level of control over your own will. Second Corinthians 10:5 puts it this way: "Casting down imaginations, and every high thing that exalteth itself against the knowledge of God, and bringing into captivity every thought to the obedience of Christ" (KJV).

That's a very deliberate and thoughtful decision on my part, and I am blessed to have such a strong will to help keep me committed to my resolve. The term *submission* takes on a whole new meaning when I realize the only one I am completely surrendered to knows and loves me best and would never take advantage of my trust. Churches, denominations, pastors, and religious leaders all might be tempted to exploit me, but Jesus Christ will forever be the one true foundation, and I can confidently build my life around my submission to him.

Obedience

Obedience may well be the most misunderstood term of all when it comes to how a strong-willed woman perceives a personal relationship with Jesus Christ. I've maintained for several years that the old hymn "Trust and Obey" should be rephrased. Instead of "trust and obey," I like "Trust and Comply." To me, *comply* means I obey because I have a choice. So I would sing the song as, "Trust and comply, and I won't ask why—I'll be happy in Jesus if I trust and comply." My suggestion is somewhat tongue-in-cheek, of course, since obedience—as referred to by Christ—always implies a choice. God has never forced me to obey him, and he never will. But obedience *is* a requirement for a deep and personal relationship with Jesus Christ. If I have repented and submitted my will to him, I can't just do whatever I want to do.

Again, as strong-willed women, we often think of obeying someone as becoming a penitent child meekly accepting the stern instruction of an authoritarian parent. But that's not it at all! Obedience to Christ is not a weak, gutless reaction to someone telling us what to do. It is the willingness to listen and follow the voice of God, the voice of the one I trust more than anyone else in the world. It takes courage to step out and do what God tells us to do. Obedience to God can be the most exhilarating and challenging thing we'll ever do. It's a bold adventure—our lives lived on the edge of eternity.

Repentance requires a firm decision to turn our lives around; submission takes daily discipline to stay firmly and unshakably surrendered to Christ; obedience demands a vigorous and energetic commitment to strike out into the unknown and be willing to conquer the impossible. Wow—that sounds like Christianity was tailor-made for those of us with strong wills!

In Her Own Words

I live in Israel where life is very difficult. It is my obedience to God (because I know this is where I am to be for now) that helps my strong will kick in and say, "Okay, keep going; God says in his Word that he gives us everything we need to do his work." Some days I can't believe it's possible to go on. I will say to the enemy: "I read the Book and I know how the story ends, and you do not win; I do!" I have grown more in the Lord in the last nine years, than in all my life. (I'm forty-eight.) I know God is real and he is with me! What an exciting thing to know in your heart! What a privilege to serve Jesus! I look forward to the day he says, "Good and faithful servant."

—ANONYMOUS

In Her Own Words

An example of working things through is coming to such peace through Christ and realizing I can truly trust him to be in charge. He's just about the only "person" I can totally collapse on like that.

—ANONYMOUS

We're a Part of Something Greater Than All of Us

As a strong-willed woman, one of the things I've always respected about God is that he doesn't follow my rules. I admit, I do want others to follow my rules, but I just couldn't respect God if he went along with me most of the time. Even during the times I feel frustrated with God's timing or a perceived injustice, I inwardly feel so relieved that I can trust in one who sees and knows everything when I can see only a tiny part.

I love watching something happen that could only have been God, since all other possibilities simply weren't an option. I love it when someone comes up to me after a seminar and tells me her life has been changed because of something she read in one of my books. You see, that has to be God; I simply don't have that kind of power or control over anyone. As soon as I begin to feel that any of my success is because of me, I believe it will quickly fade. I am only a very small part of a very big picture, and I find it so exciting to be involved in the work of an almighty God. Instead of feeling like it's a big sacrifice to give my strong will to Christ, it feels like the most natural thing in the world. Eugene Peterson puts it this way:

The easiest thing in the world is to be a Christian. What is hard is to be a sinner. Being a Christian is what we were created for. The life of faith has the support of an entire creation and the resources of a magnificent redemption. The structure of this world was created by God so we can live in it easily and happily as his children. The history we walk in has been repeatedly entered by God, most notably in Jesus Christ, first to show us and then to help us live full of faith and exuberant with purpose. In the course of Christian discipleship we discover that without Christ we were doing it the hard way and that with Christ we are doing it the easy way. It is not Christians who have it hard, but non-Christians.[2]

What an incredible opportunity we have to participate in this grand divine plan! I don't know about you, but I want to be firmly in the center of God's plan for my life so that my life can fit firmly into the center of *his* plans for the world. It just doesn't get better than this!

The Unexpected Joy of Obedience

Who would have thought that by giving up my own will to Christ I would actually be able to accomplish more than I ever dreamed possible? At first, it almost seemed like a duty—repent, submit, obey. But something wonderful happened when I actually started to walk that narrow path. Rather than grudgingly doing what God wanted me to do, I suddenly discovered that when I listen and do as he says, my life is full of joy and peace. There's no shortage of trials and tribulations, of course, but I am continuously amazed at the blessings he brings about if I'll just stay obedient to him.

In Her Own Words

I have a hard time relying on the Lord because often I feel I can do it myself. (Rotten attitude, I know.) Perhaps situations are in my life to teach me to rely on him more. Situations humble me, not because I'm pious but because I'm reminded again and again how good God is. I see blessings that are not directly related to me. For instance, I work like crazy to set up something at vacation Bible school, and then something else altogether flourishes spiritually (the one aspect I barely worked on, or that someone else worked on). But then I smile and think, "Thank you God for teaching me that you're Lord and I'm not."

—Anonymous

There have been so many times during the years when my business should have just gone under, when my family should have just fallen apart, when my plans should have just collapsed. When I started my journey of faith in Christ, I had no idea what a pleasure it would be to watch him take care of every aspect of my life. I thought I'd have to use my own strength to stay true; I thought it would be so hard to find the time and energy to live a life of faith. But the more I obey, the more grace he gives me to keep doing what he wants me to do. Our pastor puts it so well when he says, "When we don't pray, we see what *we* can do; when we *do* pray, we see what God can do."

Several years ago, I had really reached the end of my rope financially. It was time to "fish or cut bait." To go forward with our small business would mean a highly risky venture into retail sales and hiring more employees to maintain the bookings and associated tasks. We didn't have the money to go on, and yet to stop would mean giving up what I thought for sure God wanted me to do. I didn't know which direction to take, and God wasn't sending any paper airplanes down to me with answers written on them. I prayed for guidance, but nothing obvious appeared. I went to church that Wednesday night, and the pastor said he felt led to share a story with us.

He was a young pastor in one of his first churches, and it was growing like crazy. He and his church board were excited, but they all agreed it would be necessary to hire an associate pastor. They prayed about it, voted on it, and decided they would wait for the extra offerings to come in so they could hire the new associate. Weeks passed, and no additional offerings were received.

The young pastor was discouraged and overburdened with work, so he sought out his friend and mentor, a semiretired preacher and evangelist. "I don't understand," said the young pastor. "In Philippians, there is the promise that God shall supply all your needs. We have a desperate need; we've prayed about it; we've claimed the promise—but God still hasn't supplied the need."

The older clergyman nodded sympathetically, then asked what seemed like a ridiculous question. "Have you hired the associate?"

The young pastor was surprised. "No, of course not—we don't have the money for it."

The older man replied gently, "Son, you don't have a need. If you've prayed through on this and you believe God wants you to do it, hire the associate. Then you'll have a need, and God can meet it. He isn't in the business of hedging your bets or making sure you have a safety net."

I'll never forget that story or the impact it had on me that night and the rest of my life. Obedience cannot be accomplished without faith, and faith doesn't come with guarantees or contingency plans. That Wednesday night, I took a deep breath, a big gulp, stepped out, and defined my need. I don't think I need to tell you how faithful God has been and continues to be in my life. My strong will only helps me stay more firmly committed to my relationship with Jesus Christ and keeps me constantly aware of what joy there is in unconditional obedience to God.

I know your life has a story, probably much more dramatic than mine. But one thing we strong-willed women can agree upon together: when we give ourselves 100 percent to God, he never disappoints us with the results. Regardless of hardship or trouble, our faith in God and our resolve to live for him are undeniably and irrevocably set. Aren't you glad you have that kind of strong will?

chapter 10

Strong-Willed Women in Crisis

Anyone who meets a testing challenge head-on and manages to stick it out is mighty fortunate. For such persons loyally in love with God, the reward is life and more life.
—James 1:12

I bumped into Connie at the store and had to do a double-take. She greeted me warmly, but her hug was weak and her eyes had a faraway look in them.

"Connie, are you okay?" I asked.

She shook her head. "No, not okay, but I'm working on being better."

Connie, a Christian, is one of the most strong-willed women I've ever met. I've known her for years, and she too is a former street cop. She's been through a lot, and she's always fought like crazy to stay upbeat and strong. Among other things, she's been through childhood molestation, parental divorce, her own divorce and remarriage, a failed business, and a blended family that includes two rebellious teenagers who didn't grow up with her. Through the years, she and I have compared notes on being a strong-willed Christian woman, and we've both agreed it was only her megadose of strong will that has allowed her to survive what she's experienced in her first forty years of life. She's always had fire in her eyes and an almost electric energy coursing through her veins.

But now she was alarmingly subdued and quiet, and I almost didn't recognize her. We didn't have a lot of time to talk, but Connie told me she had started on medication for depression. "I'm just so sad most of the time," she admitted. "I'm hoping this makes me feel better soon."

Connie—on medication for *depression?* Never in a million years would it have occurred to me that she could get to the point of needing that kind of help. I had to run, but I assured her I would call soon and we'd have coffee when she had time.

"Oh, call anytime," she said matter-of-factly. "I'm available at home almost every day now."

Okay, now I know something's really wrong. Connie is never at home! She's always been on the run between her business, her real-estate remodeling project, her kids' school, projects at church, and so on. We parted ways, and I couldn't help noticing how her posture made her look resigned and defeated.

Even the strongest-willed woman has her limits. No matter how hard we try to pretend that nothing can daunt us, the truth is that no one is immune to discouragement or depression. I do believe that Connie has a better chance than many in her situation, because she is not only a very strong-willed woman but also is dedicated to Christ. She is working with a Christian counselor, and despite her depression, she is determined to weather the storm. If I know her like I think I know her, she will do whatever it takes, and she'll make it. But if this kind of thing can happen to Connie, it can happen to any strong-willed woman anywhere. As much as we hate to admit it, we are as susceptible to crisis as anyone else. What we *do* in that crisis, however, can make all the difference in the world.

Whose Crisis?

When I asked my Strong-Willed Women focus group to discuss how to hold up during times of crisis, everyone quickly volunteered practical and positive coping strategies for staying on top of virtually any situation. As our discussion progressed, though, we discovered that all of us were referring to somebody else's crisis, never our own. We took a piece of paper and charted the differences between how we deal with someone else's trouble and how we tackle ours.

Here's a sample of what our chart looked like:

How Do We Respond to Crisis?	
Someone Else's	*Our Own*
Take charge	May avoid confronting it; nothing's wrong
Take action	Often don't admit it to ourselves or anyone else
Become involved	May refuse to admit weakness or inadequacy
Deal with it quickly and effectively	Frequently take on other projects to distract us
Doing something is better than nothing	Want to deal with it on our own terms

---

In Her Own Words

I have healed relationships and started other ones off much better by realizing I need not try to control everyone else, only myself.

—ANONYMOUS

There's a bit of a contrast, wouldn't you say? Most of us admitted we don't like dealing with our own traumatic situations, as we are reluctant to face the fact we are not in control. After all, with our strong will, we should certainly be able to outlast, outthink, and outsmart just about anything life can throw our way, right? Even in cases of abuse, domestic violence, or criminal attacks, we struggle even to use the word *victim* because it sounds so weak, so helpless. We should be stronger than this, we think. This wouldn't have happened if I'd been smarter or sharper or better. But the fact is, bad things are bound to happen to even the strongest and most determined woman. It's how we respond that sets us apart. It's who we turn to in times of crisis that determines the final outcome. And here's where we really need our strong will, not to grit our teeth, pull ourselves up by our bootstraps, and tough it out but to place our lives squarely in the care of our Creator, no questions asked.

The Greatest Challenge

In Luke 10:19–20, Jesus said, "See what I have given you? Safe passage as you walk on snakes and scorpions, and protection from every assault of the Enemy. No one can put a hand on you.

All the same, the great triumph is not in your authority over evil, but in God's authority over you and presence with you. Not what you do for God but what God does for you—that's the agenda for rejoicing."

The greatest challenge for the strong-willed woman in a crisis is not the crisis itself but the relinquishment of control and authority to God. We want to handle it ourselves; we don't want to appear weak or unable to take care of our own affairs. But it seems that God has completely different definitions of strength and weakness.

It was Valentine's Day, and my husband had decided to accompany me on my business trip to Los Angeles, turning it into a

---

In Her Own Words

When I became pregnant at twenty-five and was still doing drugs, I knew that I had some decisions to make. Because of my strong will, I did not accept God until after my daughter was born (and nonaddicted, thank God!). I knew then that God was giving me a chance to take care of one of his precious gifts. Me? Something had to be done or I would be no good to this baby or to myself. Drug addiction is one of the hardest things to overcome. There are usually relapses and a long life of misery and desperation. I have been lucky now to be clean and sober for ten years! However, I know that if I didn't have the strong will and the "stick-to-it-ness" and, of course, Jesus in my life, I never would have made it this far.

—CHRISTINE GRUBER

---

weekend getaway. We flew into the Los Angeles airport early in the afternoon and boarded the car rental van. John had made reservations at an expensive and romantic restaurant that evening, and we were anxious to get to our hotel and change. As we got to the car lot, I grabbed a suitcase in each hand and started down the stairs of the van. The last stair was very steep, and my foot slipped off the edge. As my weight shifted, the suitcases and I fell against my left wrist, and in that instant, my life was altered forever. I had the first surgery on the broken wrist that evening, and the second surgery two weeks later. After two months in a cast, the doctors determined the wrist had not healed properly. Several months later, they operated again, resetting the wrist using a bone graft, a metal plate, and several screws and pins. As the deadline for this manuscript drew near, I found myself once again spending several weeks in a constricting cast, typing with one hand. In all likelihood, the wrist will never again be whole and right.

For almost a year, I struggled to come to terms with my frustrating limitation. One day I was standing in line at the pharmacy. I clumsily propped my cast on the counter as I signed for it, and the clerk sympathized with me when I balanced the paper and pen to sign with one hand. "That must be so hard!" she said. I nodded, but a voice behind me said, "You'll get used to it." I turned to find a man with one hand in his pocket and the other hand . . . Well, he didn't have the other hand. His shirtsleeve was neatly tucked in at the waist, and his arm was gone from his shoulder. Okay, Lord, I get your point! I may not have full use of my left arm, but I do have the arm. It has slowed me down, interfered with my work, and caused me pain and discomfort. I have to admit I have found myself wishing the whole accident had never happened. But it did, and I can't change that.

What *can* I do? I can focus my strength of will on what God wants me to do in spite of adversity or trials. I can find out what God can accomplish through me when I can't be strong on my own. I love the verses in 2 Corinthians 12:7–10:

> So I wouldn't get a big head, I was given the gift of a handicap to keep me in constant touch with my limitations. Satan's angel did his best to get me down; what he in fact did was push me to my knees. No danger then of walking around high and mighty! At first I didn't think of it as a gift, and begged God to remove it. Three times I did that, and then he told me,
>
> > "My grace is enough; it's all you need.
> > My strength comes into its own in your weakness."
>
> Once I heard that, I was glad to let it happen. I quit focusing on the handicap and began appreciating the gift. It was a case of Christ's strength moving in on my weakness. Now I take limitations in stride, and with good cheer, these limitations that cut me down to size—abuse, accidents, opposition, bad breaks. I just let Christ take over! And so the weaker I get, the stronger I become.

Handling Personal Crises

As you know, there are all kinds of crises, and every strong-willed woman deals with crisis in her own way. Some get physical—working out, running, doing any exercise that pushes their bodies to the limit and crowds out other immediate concerns. Others take a quick nap, watch a favorite television show, or read a book, all of which can give just a little breathing room before they tackle an overwhelming task. I personally find myself doing a little "therapeutic shopping," with or without actually buying

In Her Own Words

My strong will got me into some deep trouble. How hard it was with my ultra-strong will to admit I needed help. I didn't need anyone or anything. Needing someone or something was a sign of weakness, and I was strong, right? This frightened, terrified, poster child for lost souls wondered if even God could help. I went through many years of depression and inner pain before I realized that asking for help proved you were strong. I learned I was a million times stronger than I ever imagined, with God's help.

—MKMKSMITH

anything. Regardless of our individual methods, however, we do seem to find common ground when it comes to how we view most stress and crisis situations.

We Tend to Not Talk about It

Many strong-willed women are reluctant to express their worries or concerns even to their closest circle of friends. After all, we are typically the ones who help others; how would it look if we turned up on the receiving end? It often isn't so much a matter of pride as it is of reluctance to bother someone with something we feel we should be able to handle ourselves.

I was so blessed to have my mother nearby when our twin sons were born. That whole first year of their lives is almost a blur to me, and yet I remember clearly what helped me cope best. Besides my husband and my parents, several women from our church just showed up with food, thoughtful cards, gifts, and welcome conversation. Just about everyone I knew had told me,

"Call me if I can do anything for you," but somehow I could never bring myself to actually call anyone. I can't tell you how grateful I was to have several friends just call me and say they were bringing something or coming to clean the house.

We can't always count on others reading our minds, and I am working on getting better about asking for what I need. But I have to tell you that the people in my life who have always meant the most to me are the ones who never make me put my requests into words.

We Believe Any Crisis Is Temporary

Every strong-willed woman I know seems to put a positive spin on adverse circumstances when the chips are down. Perhaps it's because we need to move forward and take action instead of indulging in self-pity or being paralyzed by the overwhelming needs of a traumatic situation. Growing up, I heard my mother give a familiar reply to those who said they were doing well "under the circumstances." "What are you doing *under* the circumstances?" she would ask. As a strong-willed woman, I refuse to accept that a crisis in the present will last long into the future.

Even in an event as horrible as the World Trade Center tragedy, we saw people moving immediately from being stunned to becoming unflinching rescuers. The long-term effects of that terrorist attack will forever change us, but the crushing blow to our country was temporary, largely due to the strong will and determined nature of her citizens. The worst moment of a crisis can paralyze us, but compared with our promise of eternal life, it's a temporary condition. We will not be defeated or permanently discouraged, for our hope lies firmly in the lordship of

Jesus Christ. He will never fail us, and that tells me that even the most trying times in my life will only be temporary.

We Often Believe That We Can Get Ourselves Over It

I'm not always proud of this trait in my strong-willed nature. There's a big part of me that struggles against relying on anyone or anything to help me when I'm in over my head. My friend Connie spent years denying she needed professional help, but now her survival may depend upon finding and listening to trusted medical and mental health professionals. It usually has to be pretty drastic, but even the strongest-willed woman must sometimes admit she cannot make herself better by sheer willpower. Our most important ally will always be Jesus—our closest friend, our cherished Savior, an ever-present help in time of trouble, and we do not have to carry the burden alone. But God has also called incredibly effective counselors, doctors, and other professionals and placed in them the discernment and desire for helping a soul in need of strength. In this area it is essential that the strong-willed woman find someone who understands how her mind works, who looks into her heart without judgment or surprise. But this fact remains: sometimes we just can't get over it by ourselves. If you need to seek out a professional, go armed with the knowledge of who you are and how you think. Ask God and your trusted friends to direct you to someone who will help you bring out your very best.

Strength for Today

When reading Max Lucado's book *Traveling Light,* I was struck by the truth he draws from Matthew 6:34: "Give your entire attention to what God is doing right now, and don't get worked up about what may or may not happen tomorrow. God will help you deal with whatever hard things come up when the time comes." Lucado notes:

> That last phrase is worthy of your highlighter: *when the time comes.*
>
> "I don't know what I'll do if my husband dies." You will, *when the time comes.*
>
> "When my children leave the house, I don't think I can take it." It won't be easy, but strength will arrive *when the time comes.*
>
> "I could never lead a church. There is too much I don't know." You may be right. Or you may be wanting to know everything too soon. Could it be that God will reveal answers to you *when the time comes?*
>
> The key is this: Meet today's problems with today's strength. Don't start tackling tomorrow's problems until tomorrow. You do not have tomorrow's strength yet. You simply have enough for today.[1]

That's quite a promise, and quite a challenge for those of us who often tend to shoulder the weight of the world. Lord, today let us recognize that you are in charge, and you will give us as much strength as we need for any crisis. Amen.

chapter 11

Mentoring the Next Generation of Strong-Willed Women

*We couldn't be more sure of ourselves in this—that you,
written by Christ himself for God, are our letter of
recommendation. We wouldn't think of writing this kind
of letter about ourselves. Only God can write such a letter.
His letter authorizes us to help carry out this new plan of
action. The plan wasn't written out with ink on paper,
with pages and pages of legal footnotes, killing your spirit.
It's written with Spirit on spirit, his life on our lives!*
—2 Corinthians 3:2–3

I boarded the airplane early on that Friday morning two years ago. I do a lot of flying, so I was anxious to just get settled in my seat and let everyone else board. I had a few copies of a flier for my newest book tucked into my briefcase. On the cover of the flier in big bold letters were the words, "Are You Struggling with Your Strong-Willed Child?" Inside were excerpts from the book and a synopsis of each chapter.

Before I could even put my seat belt on, I felt God's unmistakable elbow nudging me to go up to visit the cockpit. For a moment, I resisted. I'd feel silly going up there with no children in tow. What would I say? But I know better than to ignore those promptings, so I took out a flier and headed up to the front of the plane.

The captain was standing in the cockpit when I approached, so I handed him the paper, and said, "I brought you some reading material in case you get bored during the trip."

I turned to walk away, but he stopped me and motioned me into the cockpit. His eyes were intense, and he waved the flier in front of me. "How did you know to give this to *me* today?" he asked.

I looked surprised. "Why?" I countered.

That handsome, uniformed, and decorated pilot had tears in his eyes. "We have an eighteen-year-old *very* strong-willed daughter," he said. "We've had it. Monday she goes in for counseling, but that's only because the airline will pay for it. I'm through. I've never seen such a selfish, ungrateful, rebellious girl in my life." He went on to tell me about his daughter for a few minutes until it was time for me to take my seat.

Before I left, I said to him hopefully, "Well, it's good that she's agreed to go to counseling, at least."

His expression turned angry and he pointed his finger at me. "As long as she lives in my house and eats at my table, she'll do what I *tell* her to do!"

I backed up a little and said quietly. "I hate to tell you this, but she probably won't come back."

He leaned closer, the tears still fresh in his eyes. "I don't care if I never see her again the rest of my life," he said matter of factly.

I wish I could tell you I've never heard this before. I wish I could tell you this was just a man with poor parenting skills who doesn't care and doesn't know any better. But it wouldn't be true. I've talked to dozens of adults who feel the same way. They are loving, conscientious parents who are just at the end of their ropes. If there's anyone who recognizes this frustrated, harried parent, it's those of us who probably put our own folks through it already. That gives us a unique opportunity to perhaps be the one person in a family's life who *does* understand and appreciate the mind of a headstrong, stubborn, strong-willed girl.

Strategies for Mentors

Who better to mentor the younger strong-willed generation than us? I know, some of you are thinking you have enough trouble right there at home with your own strong-willed child. But you may be amazed to find out how a change in perspective will benefit you by spending a little time with someone who

---

In Her Own Words

If there was anything I'd like to say to a strong-willed woman, it would be this:

What a treasure your personality and will are toward the Lord and his work, and what an example and inspiration you can be to other women! When your will and desires are channeled in such a way that you want to be and do what God desires, there is absolutely no stopping you! Be satisfied in the Lord, grateful for who you are, and ever ready to take on the tasks that he sets before you.

—Anonymous

---

needs to know what you've learned about your strong-willed nature. There are some young strong-willed girls waiting for your guidance. Need some ideas? Let me suggest a few strategies to get you started.

Let Her Know She's Normal

Before I found out my strong will wasn't abnormal, I spent a lot of time being defensive about my right to have it. Even as I fought to the death to be myself, I secretly wondered if maybe there wasn't something wrong with me after all. Many strong-willed girls experience the same thing. What's interesting is that once we figure out we're okay, we spend less energy being defensive and have more left over to accommodate others.

Find ways to identify with your "apprentice." Share with her what you've been through, and let her know she's not alone in her feelings. Remind her that in the sisterhood of strong-willed women, we actually pride ourselves on not fitting in with the "normal" crowd. We look for ways to be unique and special, and we pride ourselves in our ability to "think outside the box." The more you emphasize the positive aspects of standing out in a crowd, the better chance you'll have of convincing her not to do it in an unacceptable or destructive way.

Help Her Find Her Strengths

Help her find her strengths, even when they get her in trouble. I found out years ago that most of us get hired for the very same traits and characteristics that got us in trouble in school. Most human resources directors are looking for employees with good social interaction skills, independent thinking skills, and a high energy level. None of these are usu-

In Her Own Words

I was the best athlete, even better than the boys. I was strong and I knew it. I don't think the boys liked it. Because not only was I physically strong, I would tell it like it is, and kids didn't like that. I was considered tough. I guess it scared the boys. My mom used to say I was built like a brick shipyard. Imagine being a girl growing up with that image in your head. Girls were supposed to be petite and helpless. I was boisterous and sassy. My mouth has always gotten me in trouble! I have had to dole out many an apology for an opinion I absolutely had to impart on another, or for angry words that popped out without thought. I definitely learned how to ask forgiveness at an early age!

—MKMKSMITH

ally encouraged when you're going to school! When it comes to the strong-willed child, a lot of what she does best is not considered an asset when she's young. Her mind works quickly, looking for angles and figuring out how to manipulate a situation to her advantage. She's usually very good at the letter of the law ("You said don't jump off *that* chair."), and the ever-present "gift" of sarcasm can earn her the title of "smart mouth." It can be a delicate matter to help her use her wit and humor without getting in trouble for it.

If she's just said something outrageous and inappropriate, try saying, "Whoa—that was a good one! You are the master of a quick comeback. I think you and I both know it was inappropriate, and I can't let you get by with it. But I love how your mind works! If we can just figure out how to use that in ways that won't get you in trouble . . ." It takes a bit of the sting out of the punishment when she realizes you can see beyond her bad behavior and recognize something that will be a great asset to her in the future.

I often remind mothers of strong-willed children they need to smile at them more. When you're a strong-willed child, people just aren't that happy to see you walk into a room! Pretty soon, you can get a complex, thinking no one really knows how good you can be, because they're always expecting the worst. Help your strong-willed protégé get a firm handle on her strengths, and you'll find she'll start to use them in ways that will get your approval.

Give Her Opportunities to Succeed

Even very young strong-willed children don't like to feel they are in a position of weakness by admitting they don't know something. I told the story in my first book, *The Way They Learn,* of a wise homeschool mom who had to figure out how to motivate her bright, strong-willed son to learn to read. He was avoiding the whole thing because he really felt he should already know how to do this. He hated the thought of starting at square one and feeling stupid.

His mom took him shopping for a puppet, and they brought home Molasses the Moose. He and his mother together taught Molasses the Moose how to read, and that puppet was a very fast learner! The chances are good that your strong-willed pupil is eager to assume leadership. Try finding as many ways as possible to let her be in charge of something or someone. Speaking as a former teacher, I always mastered my subjects best when I kept teaching them to others. If your strong-willed child's strengths are in organization, give her the job of organizing what she must learn. If her strength is talking, find ways she can talk through her work or assignments as she does them. The possibilities are endless, and it won't take you long to figure out how to make the most of her natural abilities—after all, it takes one to know one!

Help Her Stay Grounded in the Word of God

This can be tough, since it's not uncommon to find strong-willed kids bored with Bible studies or Sunday school. It doesn't have to be that way, and in many churches you'll find some very creative and compelling teaching suggestions. If you are mentoring a strong-willed child, you don't need to be a formal teacher or church worker to introduce her to some motivating and inspiring ways to hide God's Word in her heart. Again, use your own knowledge of what works and what doesn't when it comes to reading and learning about the Bible. Make sure she wants to learn more before you find the tools for doing it. Once she has committed to a desire to stay close to God and study his Word, you and she can explore different methods together. Encourage her to stay accountable to someone, even if it's not you. Don't pressure her to report to you or her parents, but get her agreement to choose and maintain an accountability partner and set her goals clearly. Ask her how she'll know she's accomplished them, and encourage her to describe what success will look like.

When it comes to studying the Bible, it's more important than ever to avoid making it a punishment. Look for ways to let her make the suggestions and discoveries. Remember, the way she learns when she is young will have a lasting impact on how willing she is to learn when she gets older and is no longer required to do so.

Love Her, No Matter What

There will be days when even the most loving parent will be fed up with that strong-willed daughter, and times when the best teacher will do something that seems totally unfair. When the chips are down and your favorite strong-willed girl feels totally hopeless, you may be the only one in her life at that moment who can reassure her she is valuable and worthwhile. You can be the best ally for her parents and teachers just by being there to remind her she is loved. As you know, at the times when you're feeling least lovable, your best chance to pull out of it is finding someone who knows exactly how you feel. It's not your job to take the place of any of her family, but you often have the sobering privilege of being the one who can throw out a lifeline she'll actually hang on to.

Speaking as a strong-willed child myself, I know we will sometimes rant and rave and push everyone away. We'll tell you we hate you and don't want you around, and we'll demand you leave and never come back. But it's just a test. You say you'll love us no matter what, and we say, "Really? What about this?" And sometimes we find out you don't really love us no matter what; you love us if we follow your rules or do what you say. Otherwise, you seem to withdraw your love, and that's devastating. We need to know someone will be there, regardless of how far and how many times we push them away. Could it be there is a strong-willed girl within your realm of influence right now who needs you to step in and provide that reassurance of unconditional love? Be careful—if you think about it and pray about it, don't be surprised at how fast God will show you the answer!

How Will We Draw More Strong-Willed Women to the Church?

I spoke to a weekend women's conference recently, and I had them take the Strong-Willed Woman quiz in chapter 1. Out of the almost three hundred women in attendance, fewer than twenty scored an eight or higher on the strong-willed scale. Everyone seemed surprised there weren't more strong-willed women participating in this well-planned annual event, but almost everyone could think of several absent friends who would have scored higher than they did on the quiz.

I just didn't have the heart to tell them why those strong-willed sisters in Christ weren't sitting beside them at the banquet tables. After all, there was absolutely nothing wrong with how they had organized and executed the whole weekend. There were craft tables and friendship circles and opportunities to do group shopping in the antique district. The choices of afternoon seminars included aromatherapy, creative stamp art, and board games. Right after lunch, there was a fashion show using many of the conference participants themselves. The decorations were beautiful and the whole program went off without a hitch. It's just that as a strong-willed woman, there was nothing that would compel me to come if I weren't the keynote attraction.

I'm looking for action, a fast-paced, entertaining speaker, and an irresistible challenge to stretch my faith and do something out of the ordinary. I don't mind your offering the stamp art seminars, but let me choose the workshop that demonstrates how I can establish or participate in a community program that will feed the hungry or minister to the homeless in the inner city. I'll sign up for the first aid course that certifies me as a front-line volunteer in a crisis or neighborhood disaster. I'd love to have a "field trip," but give me the option to do something I can't do at home—horseback riding or kayaking or hiking up a mountain at sunrise.

If you want to find ways to attract the strong-willed women in your community, use your own strong-willed friends and colleagues as resources. Ask them what would appeal to them and see if they'll agree to be on the executive planning committee for women's ministry. Once you begin to draw out the strong-willed women in your congregation, you'll find many more opportunities to reach out into the community with something substantial and appropriate for even the women who are most difficult to please. Focus on developing programs that are designed to attract younger strong-willed women—even teenagers—and then concentrate on finding ways to mentor and love them into fellowship with Christ. Remember, it takes one to know one, so cultivate bonds with strong-willed Christian women who can truly identify with their unchurched cohorts.

What's the Reward?

I know you probably wouldn't mentor a strong-willed young woman because you expected anything tangible in return, but it's natural to count the cost of spending precious time and energy on someone who isn't even a member of your family. There's a familiar saying: "You can count the seeds in an apple, but you can't count how many apples are in the seeds." I believe every strong-willed person changes the world one way or another; after all, it isn't likely that the world will change her! What a wonderful opportunity we have to step up and help shape the future of these gifted and spirited young women! I've already had the privilege of mentoring a few strong-willed women, and I want to share a note I got from one of my favorites recently:

Cindy,

Wow! When I read that e-mail you wrote . . . all I could do was fall to my knees and cry! I just had to thank God for being so gracious! I don't know what I could have possibly done to deserve meeting someone like you, but there is not a day that goes by that I don't thank him for the privilege to just know you! Just the comfort of knowing someone believes in me and thinks that the very thing everyone else seems to think will ruin my chance for success will be the key to my success (strong will) is a huge light for me. Most everyone has always thought Ashley and I would go nowhere. But deep inside my heart I knew we would. Even if something were to happen and I couldn't get my M.D., I would still have gone so far. Just to know God and follow his will is so much more rewarding than anything else! When I was up there with you, I noticed that I had never felt so close to God! And I couldn't help but think, Wow! what a wonderful vessel he chose to work through! I feel uneasy, as if God is working in my life right now. Making changes and decisions that will change my life forever. It is so hard to just let him work; I'm so used to taking care of myself, it is hard to let him take care of me. I am working on that! I am just afraid of failing! Someday you'll see—I'll repay you for your enormous amount of kindness!! I love you!

Autumn

That's what keeps me going, and do you know how I'm going to have Autumn repay me? That's right—she'll mentor someone else, and another corner of the world will change forever.

The Challenge

*Don't begin by traveling to some faroff place to convert
unbelievers. And don't try to be dramatic by tackling some
public enemy. Go to the lost, confused people right here in
the neighborhood. Tell them that the kingdom is here.
Bring health to the sick. Raise the dead. Touch the
untouchables. Kick out the demons. You have been treated
generously, so live generously.*

    *Don't think you have to put on a fund-raising
campaign before you start. You don't need a lot of
equipment. You are the equipment, and all you need to
keep that going is three meals a day. Travel light.*

                          —Matthew 10:5–10

Are you ready to share this message with other strong-willed
women? Can you think of some women in your family,
your circle of friends, or your workplace who need to hear some
encouraging words? Following these chapters, you'll find a study
guide for this book. It's intended to help small groups or outreach ministries touch a population of women we may have
largely overlooked until now. There are some powerful possibilities out there, and you may just be the one to bring the good
news. Let's do a quick review of what we mean when we refer
to godly strong-willed women:

- They are not pushy, aggressive women demanding equality or power but women with convictions of steel who have dedicated their strong wills to their Creator and Lord and seek with every fiber of their strong-willed souls to bring honor and glory to God.
- They are not weak women who have simply been through "assertiveness training." These are women with God's design indelibly inscribed on their hearts and minds, destined to use their strong wills and indomitable natures to change the world.
- Their lives are grounded in the Word of God, and their walks are filled with adventures of a faith that takes risks and holds steady under even the most relentless pressure.
- They are women who have voluntarily surrendered their strong wills to Christ, full of respect and love for a God who would never simply take their strong wills from them; they choose to live their lives in the most incredible and fulfilling relationship they will ever have.

It is my sincere desire that this book will validate the strong-willed woman in ways no one but another strong-willed woman could. It is my prayer that the ideas in these pages can be used for outreach, lifting up Christ and drawing even the strongest will back

---

In Her Own Words

My strong will doesn't get me in trouble; "I" (self) gets me in trouble. In other words, I don't lay down my life; I want my selfish desires.

—Anonymous

---

to its Creator. I believe we can make the strong-willed woman feel understood and appreciated and fill her with hope and encouragement. We will know we have succeeded if we can inspire her to continually bring out the best in her own strong-willed nature without ever compromising her relationship with Jesus Christ.

An Intriguing Idea

What if we could raise up an entire network of strong-willed women for Christ? Now that could truly create a force to be reckoned with! Even without a formal national organization, local churches could foster the growth of groups of women who form a unique and much-needed area of women's ministry. These Strong-Willed Women for Christ groups (SWWC) could reach an entirely new population of women who may not be drawn to the traditional women's meetings. As part of their fellowship, they could:

- Build one another up through the Word and help one another keep their strengths grounded firmly in Christ.
- Find ways to love, respect, and honor their husbands and families.
- Identify strengths, even in the face of what seem to be irritating weaknesses.
- Continually nurture and encourage new and younger members, helping them discover the joy of surrendering to the one who designed them and allowing him to make them wonderful examples of his grace and determination.
- Look for ways to help answer the prayers of others, specializing in creative and resourceful thinking to accomplish sometimes almost impossible tasks.

Why Would This Group Appeal to Strong-Willed Women?

- We can be instrumental in saving relationships, careers, and even lives by helping the world understand that a strong will is not a negative trait when it is used for a positive purpose.
- We can form an unbreakable chain of friendship and relationships by understanding how each other's minds work and by accepting our strong will on God's terms, not our own.
- We can support each other, finding and reminding an accountability partner of ways to show love and respect to our husbands and children, even when we are too busy think about it.

Are you getting more ideas yet? The possibilities are endless, and the prospects of reaching strong-willed women with the message of Christ are exciting and very important. If you are serious about focusing on this area of women's ministry, find a core group of strong-willed women who are committed to Christ and dedicated to sharing the good news with others in a way their minds are designed to understand it. Use your "panel of experts" to guide you through the whole process, and then to monitor and evaluate the effectiveness of your approach. There's no doubt this will be an exhausting undertaking; after all, the pace will be fast, the activities intense, and the results often unpredictable. In the end, however, your best efforts won't have to come from your own strength and insight. Remember, if you lift up Christ, *he* will draw all men (and strong-willed women) unto him. Whew! That's a huge load off *our* shoulders! There's a world full of strong-willed women out there; let's go tell them the wonderful news about the God who created and designed them to be just who they are when they bring honor and glory to him! I don't believe you read this book by accident. I pray that God will use you to draw other strong-willed women to him. I hope you will let me know you're out there and keep in touch with me. May God richly bless you and help you to use your strong will to draw the world to him.

Study and
Discussion Guide

Chapter 1: Who Is the Strong-Willed Woman?

Although this study and discussion guide is designed to be used with groups of strong-willed women, you'll have a great time among *all* the women in your church or group as you compare notes.

Since the whole first chapter is dedicated to identifying individual levels of strong will, I suggest that everyone take and score the Strong-Willed Woman quiz (p. 22). Then briefly discuss the descriptions of what group members have in common. To do this, I suggest you divide into small groups.

Group Activity

You may choose to divide into groups according to the scores on the quiz (0–3, 4–7, 8–10, 11–12), or you may prefer to have women identify their level of strong will and group accordingly: low, medium, or high. Give the three or four groups between ten and fifteen minutes to answer the following questions. Have each group designate a spokesperson who will record the group's responses and share them later with the larger group.

Explain that each small group should come to consensus before writing answers; encourage them not to record answers when there is not agreement among all group members. Remind everyone that each group will include different personalities, learning styles, and temperaments. In this activity, we are focusing primarily on level of strong will.

Three Questions to Answer with Consensus as a Group

1. What's the best way to change my mind about something?
2. How does someone get me to take no for an answer?
3. What makes a risk worth taking?

Each group might write its responses on a large piece of chart paper, an overhead transparency, or simply read it from notes. When the groups are sharing their answers, I suggest you start with the group with the lowest strong-will score, contrast with the highest, and end with the middle group or groups, to see if it indeed is balanced between the two extremes. Open the floor for discussion after each group has shared, and ask the others to point out the most striking similarities or differences between the responses. This is also a good time for those in opposite groups to ask questions about how a group thinks and why they do what they do. Emphasize the positive aspects of being in each group, and steer the discussion away from critical comments. Look for ways to celebrate the strong will in everyone, regardless of how much or how little is identified.

Individual or Group Questions

The following questions are best answered individually, but they may also be used as group discussion starters.

1. What is your Strong-Willed Woman Quotient (p. 23)? Do you agree or disagree with the score? Why?

2. When people have called you strong willed (or just plain stubborn), what did they mean by it? What kinds of things were you doing or saying that earned you that label?

3. What strong-willed traits that got you in trouble when you were younger have actually become assets now that you're older? Think of specific examples.

4. If it hadn't been for your strong will, how would your life be different than it is now? Think of a specific example.

5. Of all the descriptions beginning on page 25, which three best describe you? If possible, give an example for each.

6. On the top half of a blank sheet of paper, write down three positive aspects to your strong-willed nature. Then at the bottom, take the same three things and write down what could happen if they were taken to the extreme. (For example: Top: my die-hard determination to win. Bottom: I could become ruthless, prepared to win at all costs.)

7. Briefly describe what we need to know about you and your strong will in order to understand you better.

A Thought

Even the best in us
can become the worst in us
without Christ at home in us!

Chapter 2: Strong Will— It's Not Always What You Think!

1. If you were to identify the areas of your life in which your strong will tends to be most misunderstood, what would they be? Why?

2. Myth 1: a strong will is automatically a negative trait. How does your life prove this statement is a myth?

3. What favorite role model, alive or dead, famous or not, stands as a shining example of how a strong will can be the most positive trait a person could have?

4. Myth 2: strong-willed women are men-haters. Can you think of examples of times when a man has felt you used your strong will in a negative, personal attack against him? Is there any possibility he was justified in thinking that?

5. Is it possible to be a "feminist" and not be a man-hater? What would a "Christian feminist" be like?

6. How could a strong-willed woman foster a positive and healthy relationship with men, both personally and professionally?

7. Myth 3: Describe your own "bad girl" experiences. Do you believe it's necessary to be really bad in order to be really good? Why or why not?

8. Myth 4: strong-willed women can't be quiet or compliant. When does your more compliant and cooperative side usually come out? Would most people who know you consider you to be strong willed, or would they be a bit surprised to find out you scored so high on the quiz?

9. Myth 5: strong-willed women can't take orders or work for someone. Think of a job you've had where you had to follow orders, be subservient, or obey without questions. Were you successful? Why or why not? What does this say about your use of strong will?

10. What one other myth could you add to the list given in this book? Why is it a myth?

Chapter 3: What's the Difference between Strong Willed and Compliant?

1. There's a big difference between "compliant" and "weak willed." Think of someone you know and love whom you consider to be compliant in the best sense of the word—providing support, helping you fulfill your vision, coming alongside you to encourage and cheer you on. In two columns compare characteristic attitudes and actions of a "weak willed" person and your compliant friend:

My Compliant Friend	A Weak-Willed Person

2. How can you tell when a person is being a "pushover"?

3. What's the biggest difference between the way you argue and the way your compliant friends argue?

4. How are we as strong-willed women most likely to offend (usually not deliberately) our compliant counterparts?

5. What characteristics of our compliant family members, friends, and colleagues cause us to respect them?

6. Can you think of a few examples of compliant women who changed the world?

Chapter 4: Strong-Willed Women on Their Own

1. Have you had any "scary" experiences with singles groups? Describe and explain.

2. As a single woman, what criticisms or warnings did you hear most often from your friends and family? How did you defend yourself?

3. If you are a single woman older than forty, what options do you see for having or caring for children if you marry late?

4. Just for fun, write a classified ad, either for yourself or a single friend of yours.

5. At the top of a lefthand column write the word *acceptance*. At the top of a righthand column write *resignation*. Under each heading write words or phrases you see as causes, effects, and synonyms. Whether you are single or married, which column better describes your life? What does this say about your strong will?

6. Father ten Boom suggested that Corrie "ask God to open up another route for that love to travel." If you have known the pain of lost love, what other route might your energy possibly take?

7. In what ways can the church encourage—but not take advantage of—strong-willed single women as they serve the church and the wider community?

Chapter 5: Strong-Willed Women and the Men Who Love Them

1. What were your expectations of marriage in the beginning?

2. What kind of partner did you picture your husband being?

3. What do you think your husband's expectations were of you as a wife?

4. What statements or questions would you add to your own personal "nuclear battles" warning list? (p. 75)

5. Have you discovered any effective "disarming" techniques for your own nuclear battles?

6. How do you usually apologize to your husband? Is he satisfied with that?

7. Name one area of your marriage over which you have control that you would like to change.

8. What actions are you willing to take to make the above change happen?

9. In the illustration by Carl Windsor (p. 76), the happily married wife of fifty years decided to deliberately overlook at least ten faults of her husband to keep harmony in her relationship. Can you name at least three irritating things about your husband that you would be willing to consciously overlook to keep your marriage peaceful and happy?

10. What's your best advice to a man who plans to marry a strong-willed woman?

Chapter 6: Strong-Willed Moms Who Got the Kids They Deserved

1. Can you think of at least one recent example of hearing your strong-willed child say something you know he or she picked up from listening to you? Is this positive or negative?

2. When you were a child, what did you get in trouble for most often?

3. If you're being honest, which of the things that irritate you about your strong-willed child are also what irritated your parents about you as a child?

4. Are you happy with the current relationship between you and your strong-willed child? If not, what do you think it would take to improve it?

5. Because "it takes one to know one," can you identify any areas of conflict between you and your strong-willed child that can be attributed to the two of you sharing the same level of steely determination?

6. Can you think of an example for any or all of the following reasons you might have gotten in trouble as a kid?

    A. Lack of interest
    B. Lack of motivation
    C. Perceived lack of trust
    D. Lack of control
    E. Perceived lack of authority

7. If you were to choose just one conflict to resolve between you and your strong-willed child, what would it be and where would you start?

Chapter 7: Strong-Willed Women in the Workplace

1. Are you in the right job? Why or why not?

2. What's the worst job you can remember having? How did you survive?

3. Have you faced any of the "greatest challenges" mentioned in this chapter?

    A. Dictatorial boss
    B. Inflexible schedules
    C. Working with those who don't share your enthusiasm
    D. Working with those who are slow or lack ambition

4. Have you found your calling? What would your ideal job be? If you don't know, how will you find out?

5. What resources right in your own church or friendship circles could you turn to for help in your career search?

Chapter 8: Strong-Willed Women in Leadership

1. What do you see as the primary difference between men and women in leadership?

2. What positive methods could strong-willed women use to demonstrate our competence without making it seem as if we're just forcing our way in because we want "equal rights"?

3. Is there ever a time when the bar should be lowered in order to accommodate women in leadership?

4. Think of your experience. What specific situations have you encountered in which a woman could have been a more effective leader than a man, or vice versa?

5. Although each strong-willed woman exhibits a unique combination of talents and abilities in leadership, in general what do we offer in the workplace?

6. What, if any, leadership challenges are unique to church ministry? Are there certain areas where being a strong-willed woman leader might not be appropriate?

7. When we are in a position of leadership, especially when it involves managing others, how can our strong will potentially get in the way of doing the best possible job?

Chapter 9: Strong-Willed Women and Their Relationship with God

1. What or who brought you to Christ?

2. Which relationships in your life have most influenced you in your walk with God?

3. Are there relationships where you stayed close to God in spite of them, not because of them?

4. When it comes to the word *repentance,* how could it be misunderstood by strong-willed women? What does it personally mean to you?

5. How would you describe your own "submission" to Christ in a way that wouldn't sound offensive to a non-Christian strong-willed woman?

6. Why is the word *obey* often so difficult for a strong-willed woman to accept? What would personally make the concept of obedience to Christ more appealing to you?

7. Can you think of a vivid example from your life where you experienced that "unexpected joy of obedience"?

8. When it comes to sharing the gospel, especially with other strong-willed women, what do you believe are the most important considerations for determining the methods of delivery?

9. Think in terms of strong-willed women and their positive influence on history. What specific biblical characters come to mind? What lessons do you learn from them?

10. As briefly as possible, describe why you personally surrendered your strong will to Jesus Christ.

Chapter 10: Strong-Willed Women in Crisis

1. Why, as strong-willed women, would we rather solve someone else's crisis than our own?

2. How will you know when you've reached your limit and can no longer go on as if you have no crisis?

3. When you are feeling pressured or surrounded by crisis, what do you typically do to relieve the stress?

4. What's the best thing your family or friends can do for you when you really have your back against the wall? Do they know that's what they're supposed to do?

5. If you found yourself in a position where you needed to seek professional help or advice, what kind of counselor or medical professional would work best with you? How would you find the right person?

6. How can we recognize when another strong-willed woman has a crisis and would benefit from our help? How could we approach her without pushing her away?

7. Try to identify one or two definite "don'ts" when it comes to stepping in to help another strong-willed woman in crisis.

8. Do you think it's easier for a strong-willed woman to handle more pressure and stress than our compliant counterparts? Why or why not?

9. When the strong-willed woman finally realizes she can't get over the crisis by herself, how can we best show her she needs God?

Chapter 11: Mentoring the Next Generation of Strong-Willed Women

1. How will you be able to recognize a strong-willed young woman who could use the wisdom and direction of a strong-willed woman who has surrendered to Christ?

2. Take a moment to think about girls or young women in your life over whom you have some degree of influence. Which of them stand out as being strong willed?

3. In what ways can you reach out to women who feel there is something wrong with them because of their strong will?

4. Can you think of some effective methods for motivating the younger generation of strong-willed women to keep their lives grounded in the Word of God?

5. Chances are, your life is full already and you have very little time to spare. From a practical standpoint, what can you do to seek out and encourage your younger strong-willed sisters in Christ?

6. How will you know it's worth the time and effort you take to mentor another strong-willed woman?

7. What would your best advice be to a strong-willed woman who doesn't know why she thinks or acts the way she does?

The Challenge

1. What would a strong-willed women's ministry look like in your church?

2. Before you form any kind of strong-willed women's ministry, it's important to know how you will identify who these women are. By what nonthreatening means could you reach out and draw in the women in your church or organization who would not ordinarily respond?

3. What would motivate strong-willed women to gather in the first place?

4. How can you encourage accountability within your group?

5. Could you organize a strong-willed women's group that would specialize in accomplishing the "impossible"? Could you become a group that reaches out into the community and tackles the challenges no one else wants to face? What would your group look like? Where would you start?

Notes

Chapter 4. Strong-Willed Women on Their Own

1. Evelyn Bence, *Leaving Home* (Wheaton, Ill.: Tyndale, 1986), 56.

2. Catherine Marshall, *Beyond Ourselves* (Grand Rapids, Mich.: Chosen Books: 1961), 94.

3. Corrie ten Boom with John and Elizabeth Sherrill, *The Hiding Place* (New York: Bantam Books, 1974), 44–45.

Chapter 5. Strong-Willed Women and the Men Who Love Them

1. Carl D. Windsor, *On This Day* (Nashville: Thomas Nelson, 1989), 61.

Chapter 8. Strong-Willed Women in Leadership

1. James Thurber, "The Little Girl and the Wolf," in *Fables for Our Time and Famous Poems Illustrated* (New York: Harper Brothers, 1939), 5.

2. Dale Hanson Bourke, *Turn toward the Wind: Embracing Change in Your Life* (Grand Rapids, Mich.: Zondervan, 1995), 132.

3. Max DePree and James O'Toole, *Leadership Is an Art* (New York: Dell, 1990), quoted in Bill Hybels, Charles R. Swindoll, Larry Burkett, *The Life@Work Book: Sixteen Respected Leaders Talk about Blending Biblical Wisdom and Business Excellence* (Nashville: Word, 2000), 119.

4. Max Lucado, *America Looks Up* (Colorado Springs: Waterbrook, 2001), 49.

Chapter 9. Strong-Willed Women and Their Relationship with God

1. Eugene H. Peterson, *A Long Obedience in the Same Direction: Discipleship in an Instant Society* (Downer's Grove, Ill.: InterVarsity: 2000), 29.

2. Ibid, 115.

Chapter 10. Strong-Willed Women in Crisis

1. Max Lucado, *Traveling Light: Releasing the Burdens You Were Never Intended to Bear* (Colorado Springs: Waterbrook, 2001), 49.

Recommended Reading

Allender, Dan B. and Tremper Longman. *Intimate Allies: Rediscovering God's Design for Marriage and Becoming Soul Mates for Life.* Wheaton, Ill.: Tyndale, 1995.

Amidst practical biblical wisdom and relevant, tried-and-true strategies, there are woven many compelling real-life stories of married couples and their struggles and triumphs.

Cline, Foster and Jim Fay. *Parenting with Love and Logic: Teaching Children Responsibility.* Colorado Springs: Pinon Press, 1990.

If you want to raise kids who are self-confident, motivated, and ready for the real world, take advantage of this win-win approach to parenting. The information in this book can not only revolutionize your relationships with your children but also put the fun back into parenting!

Glenn, H. Stephen, Ph.D., and Michael L. Brock, M.A. *7 Strategies for Developing Capable Students.* Rocklin, Calif.: Prima Publishing, 1998.

Commonsense approach to helping our children become capable, significant young people who know how to think and make good decisions. The authors provide many encouraging words and practical tools for developing responsibility, self-discipline, and communication skills in children.

Higgs, Liz Curtis. *Bad Girls of the Bible and What We Can Learn from Them*. Colorado Springs: Waterbrook, 1999.

In her inimitably entertaining and practical style, Liz Curtis Higgs offers fresh and unique insights into the lives of "bad girls" like Jezebel and Delilah and shows us how even bad girls can teach good lessons.

_____. *Mad Mary: A Bad Girl from Magdala, Transformed at His Appearing*. Colorado Springs: Waterbrook, 2001.

An entertaining and compelling look at a biblical example of a strong-willed woman transformed by Christ.

_____. *Really Bad Girls of the Bible: More Lessons from Less-Than-Perfect Women*. Colorado Springs: Waterbrook, 2000.

Another entertaining and thought-provoking volume, revealing the power and grace of God through lives of the least likely "shady" women.

Keirsey, David and Marilyn Bates. *Please Understand Me: Character and Temperament Types*. Del Mar, Calif.: Prometheus, Nemesis, 1978.

This book provides a fascinating look at personality type and temperament. You'll discover how your temperament affects your success in relationships, careers, and life in general.

Markman, Howard J., Scott M. Stanley, Susan L. Blumberg. *Fighting for Your Marriage: Positive Steps for Preventing Divorce and Preserving a Lasting Love*. San Francisco: Jossey-Bass, 1994.

Learn to fight fair, enjoy each other's differences, and discuss even the most difficult issues without destructive arguments. You'll find lots of interactive exercises you can use as well as many practical and immediately useful strategies for keeping your marriage healthy.

Marshall, Catherine. *Beyond Ourselves*. Grand Rapids, Mich.: Chosen, 1961.

A classic for every woman's permanent library! Catherine Marshall shares guidance and insight through inspirational stories and recollections of her own life. You'll read this one over and over!

Peterson, Eugene. *The Message: The New Testament in Contemporary Language*. Colorado Springs: NavPress, 1993.

A refreshingly clear and often entertaining paraphrase of the New Testament that even the most reluctant reader can love!

Rivers, Francine. The Lineage of Grace Series: *Unveiled, Unashamed, Unshaken, Unspoken, Unafraid*. Wheaton, Ill.: Tyndale, 2000–2001.

An inspiring and incredibly enjoyable series of novellas dealing with the lives of five world-changing women from the Bible.

Snyder, Chuck and Barb Snyder. *Incompatibility: Still Grounds for a Great Marriage*. Sisters, Ore.: Multnomah, 1999.

A practical and humorous book that helps both husbands and wives recognize and appreciate their differences while they strengthen their marriage.

Tobias, Cynthia Ulrich. *Do You Know What I Like about You? Jump Starting Virtues and Values in Your Children*. Ann Arbor: Servant, 1997.

A celebration of the ways in which we as adults deal with children in our lives. This collection of narrative, photographs, and poetry will surely touch and inspire hearts and minds.

_____. *Every Child Can Succeed: Making the Most of Your Child's Learning Style.* Colorado Springs: Focus on the Family, 1995.

This book is filled with practical ideas for applying learning styles to motivation, discipline, and much more. Copyright-free profiles contained in the appendix can help parents and children record and summarize style strengths for every teacher.

_____. *The Way They Learn: How To Discover and Teach to Your Child's Strengths.* Colorado Springs: Focus on the Family, 1994.

An international best-seller, this entertaining and practical book should be required reading for any parent or teacher who truly wants to help their children succeed. These concepts are powerful tools for bringing out the best in every child.

_____. *The Way We Work: A Practical Approach for Dealing with People on the Job.* Colorado Springs: Focus on the Family, 1995.

An enlightening and easy-to-read resource for developing efficient communication with those with whom you work. This is a powerful plan for transforming your on-the-job relationships!

_____. *You Can't Make Me! (But I Can Be Persuaded): Strategies for Bringing Out the Best in Your Strong-Willed Child.* Colorado Springs: Waterbrook, 1999.

From the perspective of "it takes one to know one," this long-awaited book gives you incredibly accurate and valuable insights into the mind of a SWC (strong-willed child) and offers dozens of tried-and-true strategies for building positive, loving relationships with even the toughest kid without letting go of accountability or accepting any excuses.

Tobias, Cynthia Ulrich with Nick Walker. *"Who's Gonna Make Me?" Effective Strategies for Dealing with the Strong-Willed Child.* Seattle: Chuck Snyder and Associates, 1992. (45-minute video)

Focusing on the Concrete Random, strong-willed child, this video presents practical, hands-on strategies for bringing out the best in your strong-willed child. This is one you'll loan to your friends!

If you would like to contact Cynthia Tobias and her organization directly:

AppLe St. (Applied Learning Styles)
PO Box 1450
Sumner, WA 98390

www.applest.com
www.thestrongwilledwoman.com

We welcome your comments and strong-willed stories!

We want to hear from you. Please send your comments about this book to us in care of the address below. Thank you.

ZONDERVAN™

GRAND RAPIDS, MICHIGAN 49530 USA

WWW.ZONDERVAN.COM